PRAYER RUGS

TEXTILE MUSEUM
WASHINGTON, D.C.

PRAYER RUGS

Richard Ettinghausen
Consultative Chairman of Islamic Art,
The Metropolitan Museum of Art;
Professor of Islamic Art,
Institute of Fine Arts, New York University
**THE EARLY HISTORY, USE AND ICONOGRAPHY
OF THE PRAYER RUG**

Maurice S. Dimand
Curator Emeritus of Islamic Art,
The Metropolitan Museum of Art
PRAYER RUG WEAVING AREAS

Louise W. Mackie
Chief Curator, Textile Museum
CATALOGUE ENTRIES

Charles Grant Ellis
Research Associate of Rugs, Textile Museum
CONSULTANT

PRAYER RUG EXHIBITION

Textile Museum, Washington, D.C.
September 21 — December 28, 1974

The Montclair Art Museum, Montclair, New Jersey
January 20 — March 16, 1975

CONTENTS

ACKNOWLEDGMENTS

Although they occupy a significant position in the history of Islamic rugs, a comprehensive exhibition and publication of Prayer Rugs has not previously been attempted.

The publication of this group of prayer rugs, including some of the finest known examples from various geographic locations, has been an enormous undertaking. The result constitutes a major event in the history of rug scholarship, which was made possible through the splendid collaboration of many museums, scholars and collectors.

Alvin W. Pearson of the Hajji Baba Club of New York developed the plan for this exhibition. Bruce J. Westcott, President of the New York Hajji Baba Club, worked as an intermediary between authors, museums, collectors, and printers. We extend our gratitude for their enthusiastic leadership.

We are extremely grateful to the museums and private collectors for their magnanimous cooperation in lending their important rugs to the exhibition. To the National Endowment for the Arts in Washington, D.C., a Federal agency, we express appreciation for granting the matching funds which enabled us to do much more than we had originally planned. We are also extremely grateful to the following individuals for supporting the exhibition financially:

Mr. and Mrs. George O. Bailey, Jr.   Miss Jean Mailey
Dr. and Mrs. Lewis Belamuth   Mrs. Joseph V. McMullan
Mr. Walter D. Binger   Miss Margaret Mushkian
Mr. Virgil Bird, Jr.   Mr. Alvin W. Pearson
Mr. and Mrs. W.A. Chalverus   Mr. Joseph G. Reinis
Mr. and Mrs. Paul Cootner   Mr. and Mrs. John B. Shephers
Mr. and Mrs. Newton S. Foster   Mrs. Matthew C. Sullivan
Prof. and Mrs. John W. Irvine, Jr.   Mrs. Warman Welliver
Mr. Francis Keally   Mr. and Mrs. Bruce J. Westcott
Mr. and Mrs. James A. Keillor   Mr. and Mrs. Donald N. Wilber

An enormous debt is owed to the scholars who contributed time and expertise to the writing and the compilation of this catalogue — especially to Dr. Richard Ettinghausen, Consultative Chairman of the Islamic Department of the Metropolitan Museum of Art, Professor of Islamic Art at New York University, and Trustee of the Textile Museum, for his astute contribution; to Dr. Maurice S. Dimand, Curator Emeritus of Islamic Art at the Metropolitan Museum of Art, for the admirable chapters; to Charles Grant Ellis, Research Associate of Islamic Rugs at the Textile Museum, for sharing his extraordinary knowledge and being a consultant throughout the project; and to Louise W. Mackie, Chief Curator at the Textile Museum, who is the author of the catalogue entries and who was responsible for guiding all the collaborative efforts so successfully. Our thanks are also extended to the staff members of both the Montclair Art Museum and the Textile Museum who were involved in this exhibition and publication.

Katheryn Gamble   Anthony N. Landreau
Director, Montclair Art Museum   Executive Director, Textile Museum

LENDERS TO
THE EXHIBITION

Anonymous
The Dumbarton Oaks Collection
Dr. and Mrs. Murray L. Eiland
Charles Grant Ellis
Field Museum of Natural History, Chicago
The Fogg Art Museum, Harvard University
Harold M. Keshishian
The Metropolitan Museum of Art
Mrs. Frank M. Michaelian
Frank M. Michaelian
Karl F. Milde
Alvin W. Pearson
Philadelphia Museum of Art
Dr. M.A.S. de Reinis
The St. Louis Art Museum
Mrs. Harper Sibley
Jerome A. Straka
Edmund de Unger
The Walters Art Gallery

THE EARLY HISTORY, USE AND ICONOGRAPHY OF THE PRAYER RUG*

Richard Ettinghausen

Figure 1—Jean Léon Gérôme "Prayer in the Mosque of Amrou, Old Cairo." New York, Metropolitan Museum of Art (no. 87.15.130), Bequest of Catherine Lorillard Wolfe, 1887.

Of all the Near Eastern, North African and Central Asian carpets, one of the most popular types, if not perhaps *the* most popular and widely used type in the Western world, is the prayer carpet (sajjāda in Arabic). The reasons are not difficult to understand. First, the prayer carpet is attractively decorated and has an undeniable exotic charm, making it a key piece for a floor covering. Second, it is easily recognized by the indicated arch, generally assumed to symbolize the mihrab, or prayer niche, which in every mosque traditionally marks the direction to Mecca to be faced by worshipers. Third, it was made in large numbers, beginning in the 17th century, particularly in Anatolia; thus it is not too rare and can still be found in many shops. Fourth, its small size permits it to be placed in most living areas, on floors or walls, from palaces to apartments. Finally, people who could not buy a large "Oriental Carpet" can do so in the case of prayer carpets because of their accessibility, convenient size and reasonable price.

In the Mid-East, the prayer carpet has had, and still has, an aesthetic attraction quite beyond its ritual use. Therefore, it was not an accident that in 1953 the first book on carpets, brought out by the Museum of Islamic Art in Cairo and printed by the Ministry of Education Press in an Arabic and an English edition, was Mohamed Mostafa's *Turkish Prayer Rugs*. From a statement in the Preface written by Mustafa Amer, the Egyptian Director General of Antiquities at the time, it is obvious that the cultural leaders in Egypt were aware of the historic significance of this publication. It states: "This volume, in spite of its small size, will be the first on carpets in general, written in Arabic, and without doubt the first to deal with prayer rugs written in any language." The fact that the Egyptian author chose to write on a group of Turkish rugs (rather than Egyptian carpets made in his country in the 15th and 16th centuries and which can no longer be found there) is easily explained from a historical point of view: from the 19th century on, it was fashionable to use Turkish prayer carpets in Egypt. E. W. Lane confirms this fact in his *Account of the Manners and Customs of the Modern Egyptians* based on his experiences in that country between 1825 and 1835. He wrote that "sajjadas are imported from Asia Minor into Egypt and used then only by the rich to perform the salat (the ritual prayer) upon and also as saddle covers."

That the well-to-do Egyptians had a predilection for Turkish prayer carpets and regarded them as status symbols is borne out by a painting in the Metropolitan Museum of Art's collection, "Prayer in the Mosque of Amrou, Old Cairo," by Jean Léon Gérôme (1824-1904). Here, the represented scene is obviously a reflection of an experience which the artist must have had during his trip to Egypt in 1867. In the foreground an important person is standing in front of two retainers. It is this dignitary alone who performs his prayer on what is undoubtedly an Anatolian prayer rug, while ordinary mats suffice for the less affluent members of the congregation (Fig. 1).

There is, however, a more ancient testimony which establishes Egyptian interest in prayer rugs as early as late medieval times. In the second quarter of the 14th century the Moroccan world traveler, Ibn Battuta, wrote one of the earliest and most extensive accounts on conditions in Cairo. This thorough description even included information on medieval prayer rugs. The following is an excerpt from that report:

"Another of the customs of the members of the zawiya (the convent of a mystic brotherhood), is that each of them sits on his own sajjada. When they offer the morning prayer, they read the Surah of Victory (the 48th chapter of the Koran), that of Royalty (the 67th chapter of the Koran), and *Surah Ain-mim* (the 68th chapter of the Koran) after which each fakir (or dervish) is given a juz' (section) of the Koran, and in this way a complete reading of the Koran is done; then they recite praises of God. Finally these readers of the Koran do a reading in the Oriental fashion. All this is also done following the afternoon prayer. Here are [also] some of the customs that they observe regarding postulants (qadim). The postulant arrives at the monastery door where he stands (and waits), his waist bound by a girdle, and carrying a sajjada on his shoulder. His right hand holds a staff, his left a ewer (ibriq). The monastery porter (bawwab) takes the news of his presence to the servant of the zawiya who goes to greet the postulant and to ask him where he is from, in which zawiyas he has stayed during his travels, and who has been his spiritual superior (shaykh). Having satisfied himself that he (the postulant) is telling the truth, the servant invites him into the zawiya and spreads out his rug at an appropriate spot and shows him the place where ablutions are done. After the stranger makes his ablutions he retires to the place where his rug has been spread, he removes his girdle, and says a prayer of two rik'as then he greets the shaykh and his entourage and sits with them" (*Voyages*, ed. & tr. C. Defrémery and B. R. Sanguinetti, Paris, 1853. I, 72-74).

In another account the servant transports everyone's sajjada to the mosque where he spreads them out. The fakirs go to the mosque with their shaykh and (there) each one prays on his own rug. This done, they read the Koran, as is their custom; then they all return to the monastery together, again accompanied by the shaykh.

Detailed as this report is, it, unfortunately, is not specific about two important points: the material of which the Egyptian sajjada was made and what design it had, if any. It could have been a knotted or a flat woven carpet, a textile, or even a mat made of leaves. Indeed, there is one other passage in Ibn Battuta's *Voyages*, which speaks specifically of prayer rugs made from leaves of a tree similar to the palm tree, only not fruit-bearing. This is found in the account of a town in West Africa where a woolen carpet would have been uncomfortably hot. It is mentioned when the Moroccan's servants spread out a sajjada made of leaves well ahead of the arrival of their master in order to reserve a place for him in the communal prayers (*Voyages*, ed. & tr. Defrémery and Sanguinetti, IV, 422).

Thus, it is evident from the 14th century report on Cairo, that the sajjada was more than a mere implement used for the five daily prayers. It appears to have been a very personal object treated with a certain reverence which was also used to sit on for sacred functions. It is likewise significant that the postulant carried (along with his staff) just two objects of ritual significance, namely the sajjada and the ewer used for ablutions before the prayer. Both these facts — the sajjada as a sacred seat and its association with a ewer — are borne out by other evidence which will be presented later on.

II

What seems to be the earliest representation of a sajjada occurs in a manuscript of Bal'ami's Persian translation of Tabari's *History* in the Freer Gallery of Art in Washington, and shows Muhammad sitting on this type of carpet. From its style it can easily be recognized as a work of the Inju school of Shiraz which flourished from about 1330 until 1343, if not earlier (Fig. 2). In this particular section of the painting the Prophet is not seen praying, but engaged in conversations with Abu Bakr and Ali, the first and fourth

Figure 2—"The Prophet Muhammad on a Prayer Rug," Detail from a miniature in Bal'ami's Persian Translation of Tabari's *History,* Iran (Shiraz), second quarter of 14th century. Washington, D.C., Freer Gallery of Art (no. 57.16, page 157). Photograph Courtesy Freer Gallery of Art, Smithsonian Institution.

caliphs. He is clearly seated on a sajjada. The sajjada in the Inju miniature is similar to later specimens, as it, like them, is characterized by a niche-like arch. Besides a border, the only other decoration is the word "Allah" set in the apex of the arch. Although it remains uncertain which material or technique was used, the fine linear design makes it unlikely that a mat is represented. In general, it was frowned upon to decorate carpets with sacred texts, as stepping or sitting on them would have been regarded as blasphemy. This rule, as the miniature and other later examples show, apparently did not apply to sajjadas. The miniature depicts the sajjada not only as a seat of honor, but also as a kind of spiritual throne, occupied exclusively by the Prophet. Therefore, it could be ornamented with the very name of God.

A sajjada of equal significance is found in a miniature of a *Mi 'raj-nameh* (840 A.H./1436 A.D.), written in Herat and now in the Bibliothèque Nationale in Paris (Fig. 3). It shows Muhammad with Adam, Noah and David on the left and Abraham, Moses and Jesus on the right. While they are all presented in an attitude of worship, it is apparently not one taken during the ritual prayer (salat). Only the Muslim Prophet has a sajjada, which, together with his central position and the halo around his head, indicates his spiritual authority. By contrast, two other miniatures, both from a manuscript of the fable book, *Kalila and Dimnah* dated 744 A.H./1343 A.D. in the National Library in Cairo, show the sajjada with its clearly indicated arch, as it is in one instance used by a feline to serve as a seat of worldly authority (Fig. 4), while, in another, it plays the regular role of a prayer rug (Fig. 5).

Another function of the sajjada can be found in a Herati miniature, attributed to the celebrated Persian painter Behzad, but probably only by a member of his school. It illustrates a story in a manuscript of Sa 'di's *Bustan,*

13

Figure 3—"The Prophet Muhammad on a Prayer Rig with Adam, Noah and David on the Left and Abraham, Moses and Jesus on the Right," Miniature in *Mi'raj-nameh* or Apocalypse of the Prophet, in Chaghatai Turkish, Herat, 1436. Photograph from Edgard Blochet, *Les Enluminures des Manuscripts Orientaux, turcs, arabes, persans de la Bibliothèque Nationale,* Paris, 1926, Plate XXV, folio 7 recto.

Figure 4—"The Sajjada as Seat of Authority," Miniature from a Persian Translation of the Fable Book *Kalilah wa Dimnah,* Iran, 1343. Cairo, National Library.

Figure 5—"The Sajjada as Prayer Rug," Miniature from same Manuscript as Figure 4.

dated 883 A.H./1479 A.D. in the Chester Beatty Library in Dublin. Having been refused passage by the captain of a boat, a Sufi dervish has spread out his sajjada on the waters which then carries him across the broad river (Fig. 6). This is a clear implication of the supernatural or magical qualities inherent in the sajjada. Here, as in all other examples quoted earlier, the sajjada had a function which went well beyond that of a rug merely used for prayer and particularly for the act of prostration (sajd), after which it was rolled up. Even when the rug was used in a limited religious context, the special material or form of decoration evidenced the high social status of the user. It certainly does so in a Mughal miniature in the State Museum in East Berlin. In this painting, the Emperor Jahangir and one of his sons are shown praying on sajjadas while the rest share a large, ordinary carpet (Fig. 7). A recently published photograph of King Faisal of Sa'udi Arabia at prayer proves that this custom still continues in modern times. It shows him alone on a Persian carpet (which is not specifically a sajjada), while the other worshipers of less august status have to be satisfied with the wall-to-wall carpeting of the royal mosque (Fig. 8).

14

Figure 6—''The Sufi of Faryab Crosses the Broad River on his Prayer Rug,'' Miniature of the School of Behzad in a Manuscript of the *Bustan* by Sa'di, Iran (Herat), ca. 1479, folio 73 verso. Dublin, The Chester Beatty Library. Photograph Courtesy The Chester Beatty Library.

III

It is obvious that the pictorial representations of prayer rugs, especially those portraying unusual circumstances, occur later than their actual use and also postdate references to them in documents and in literature. So far this early history of the sajjada as reflected in written texts has hardly been explored. Thus I am very grateful to Professor S.D. Goitein of Princeton for having pointed out to me three such references. The first two passages occur in Geniza documents from Old Cairo which, like most of this

Figure 7—''The Emperor Jahangir and his Son Praying on two Special Prayer Rugs,'' An Album Painting, Mughal India, Period of Jahangir, ca. 1610-20. Photograph from Ernst Kühnel, *Indische Miniaturen aus dem Besitz der Staatlichen Museen zu Berlin*, Berlin, n.d., Plate (facing) II.

Figure 8—King Faisal at Prayer, Sa'udi Arabia (Riyadh), contemporary. (Photo after *People*, vol. I, no. III, March 18, 1974, pp. 14/15.)

material of a documentary nature, has been written in the Arabic language but with Hebrew characters. The first is a large order for clothes and carpets which lists two runner carpets of 24 cubits length, four exquisite, white prayer carpets (called *musallayat*, from the singular *musalla*, a word which usually means "prayer site") and asks also for two pairs of such rugs in three additional colors: indigo blue, green, and red. According to its lettering and language this document should date from the middle of the 11th century, and it seems that the order was probably sent from Kairouan in Tunisia to Cairo (University Library Collection, Cambridge, Or. 1080,77, line 27). The other reference to such musallayat occurs in the inventory of a judge which was written in A.D. 1143; here these rugs are again mentioned in connection with runner carpets (Taylor-Schechter Collection, Cambridge, NSJ 27, line 7).

Also from the 12th century but this time from Iran comes the pertinent legendary account given by the famous mystic writer Farid ad-Din 'Attar. According to him the early ascetic Hasan al-Basri (who died in A.D. 728) placed his sajjada on the waters of the Euphrates and invited the woman saint Rabi 'a al-'Adawiyya to join him there for prayer; she then threw her own prayer rug into the air and asked him in turn to perform the religious prostrations with her up there (*Tadhkirat al-Awliya*, ed. R. A. Nicholson, p. 65). This story is therefore an early example of the magic qualities which can be given to the prayer rug by the spiritual powers of saints. The passage predates the related account given in Sa'di's *Bustan* (see Fig. 6) by about one hundred years.

For the sake of completeness it should be mentioned that besides sajjada and musalla the older texts also give the term *khumra* which means a small sajjada or a prayer mat made of palm leaves and embroidered with threads. Since this designation does not occur in modern Egyptian dictionaries it seems to be no longer used in Egypt.

Short as these documents are (and thus allowing only limited deductions to be made with due caution), they nevertheless permit us to draw two conclusions which go beyond the mere fact of the early use of prayer rugs. First, they make it clear that these carpets could in certain cases be ordered by an entrepreneur. The specifications were quality ("exquisite") and color, but they did not include size, material, technique and — most puzzling for a modern connoisseur — design. The reasons for this lack of data can now hardly be fully explained. The type "musalla" was probably so standard-

17

ized that the person who commissioned these rugs could assume that the pertinent factors were well-known to the manufacturer and needed no further clarification. As to the lack of any reference to the design it could also be that the design could range within certain well-established and acceptable limits or even that there was no design at all and that size alone indicated what a musalla was, just as it was in the case of runners where only the length had to be indicated. The second inference to be drawn from the two Geniza documents is that prayer rugs had not only a certain value (hence their inclusion in a judicial inventory), but also that they were apparently objects of international trade, though in this case within the Muslim world. The wide appeal of the product which underlies this mercantile aspect is also borne out by the later importation of Anatolian prayer rugs into 17th century Holland (Fig.21), into 19th century Egypt (Fig.1), and by the use of the prayer rug scheme outside the Muslim religious sphere (no. V).

IV

A closer study of the iconography of the Anatolian sajjada reveals the various connotations attributed to it. Such a survey also demonstrates how the manipulation of these associative elements created new combinations resulting in many different varieties. This usually happened when the understanding of the original meaning had diminished. It would, of course, be best to demonstrate such developments by means of chronologically arranged examples which come from one production center or at least a single carpet-producing region. In that fashion one could follow the evolution step by step within the same category. But, due to the accidents of preservation and the comparatively limited number of pieces which have come down to us, this is not possible. One is therefore forced to visualize the development by comparing carpets from various sources and non-consecutive dates although they are nearly all Anatolian and mostly from the late 17th to the early 19th century.

The main motif of the sajjada is the symbolic arch with or without supporting columns. As stated above, this arch is generally, and it seems appropriately, assumed to represent the mihrab. This establishes a spiritual connection with Mecca and its cube-shaped shrine, the Ka'ba. Few prayer carpets are specific about the mental association between the symbolic arch and the Meccan shrine. This is not too astonishing since the mihrab itself is rarely covered with symbolic representations of the Ka'ba and even when it is, such decorations appear rather late, and then mainly in the painted ceramic tilework of 17th or 18th century Anatolia. The few examples of sajjadas which have similar schematic images of the Ka'ba are also from Anatolia and were made, again, in either the late 17th or 18th century. In one case (a Ladik carpet), there is in the central arch of a triple arcade the characteristic black square of the shrine with indications of the sacred Black Stone set into one corner as well as of the highly placed door, the water spout and the decorated band of the black cloth cover. Also, next to the Ka'ba is the low, semicircular wall called al-hatim (traditionally said to enclose the graves of Isma'il and his mother Hagar). This whole image is set in the courtyard of a mosque giving the scene an even more specific character. Another Anatolian carpet rendered in a more popular vein is less outspoken about individual features of the Ka'ba itself, but gives more details of the setting such as the various extant pavilions, the pulpit for the sermon and the suspended lamps (Fig.9).

In contrast to the rare, specific references to Mecca, there is a commonly found decorative feature which undoubtedly has a symbolic association, namely a mosque lamp suspended in the arch (nos. I, III, VI, VII & XI). At first, this motif is also surprising because mihrabs very rarely contain actual suspended lamps. They are, however, frequently shown on Iranian mihrab tiles of the 13th and 14th century and a lamp already occurs in an arch on the carved stone facade of the Mosque of al-Aqmar in Cairo dated 519 A.H./1125 A.D. Their inclusion was indubitably conditioned by a passage in the Koran, verse 35 in Sura 24: "Allah is the light of the heavens and the earth; a likeness of His light is as a niche in which there is a lamp, the lamp is in a glass and the glass is as it were a brightly shining star, lit from a blessed olive-tree."

The religious treatise, *Mishkat al-anwar* (The Niche of Lights) written by the celebrated Persian theologian and philosopher, al-Ghazali (died 1111), may very well have been the reason the lamp motif was introduced to Egyptian and Persian iconography in medieval times and then became disseminated to other Islamic lands, and later on particularly to Anatolia. In this treatise he used the words of the quoted verse of the Koran for his exposition on the mystical meaning of Allah as the Light and the guidance of the Inner Light to Allah. He thereby added to the popularity of the concept and may very well have instigated its adoption into the sacred arts, particularly in two-dimensional symbolic representations of the prayer niche on tiles, in stone and stucco carvings, and eventually on prayer carpets.

It seems significant that some carpets show a pair of candlesticks placed on an implied floor below the mosque lamp. Such candlesticks were often used in connection with actual prayer niches (Fig. 18). Clearly, the idea of a prayer niche must have existed in the carpet weaver's mind and he could have presupposed a similar interpretation of the motif by the user of the sajjada. The inclusion of the two candleholders also precludes the likelihood that the arch on the prayer carpet represents primarily a gate (real or metaphorically envisioned) leading to a higher spiritual region as a doorway of a mosque would do, since candlesticks do not occur in doorways. On the other hand, if the identification of the represented lamp with the lamp in the Koran verse is correct, the intended symbolism — the lamp standing for Allah—would also apply to the prayer carpet. This is corroborated by Muhammad's sajjada in the Inju miniature (Figs. 2 & also 18), which has the word "Allah" in the position otherwise taken by the lamp. However, even primitive renderings of the arcades (e.g., of the courtyard of the Ka'ba in the simple Anatolian carpet referred to earlier, Fig. 9) show that the area between two columns, as well as between arches, was the favorite place to suspend mosque lamps. This common motif in architectural settings may, therefore, have reinforced its use in the prayer carpet.

In the course of time the mosque lamp underwent a series of transformations. Thus, the lamp could, for instance, be multiplied (Fig. 15, no. IX). This implies that the notion of the mihrab or the identification of the lamp with "Allah," which was based on the quoted Koran verse, had been forgotten and the lamp was now conceived exclusively as a lighting fixture whose number could be increased for the greater glory of God. It was possible, however, that the opposite happened and the notion of a lamp was altogether given up. The original, realistically rendered lamp was reduced in size and clarity and eventually became an ornament suspended from the apex of the arch (Figs. 10, 11 and nos. VIII & XV); this again

19

Figure 9—Prayer Rug with representation of the Ka'ba, Western Anatolia, 18th century. Istanbul, Museum of Turkish and Islamic Art, 1632.

Figure 10—Prayer Rug, Anatolia, Gördes,19th century. Cairo, Museum of Islamic Art.

Figure 11—Prayer Rug, Anatolia, Ladik,19th century. Metropolitan Museum of Art, Gift of James F. Ballard, 22.100.61.

Figure 12—''Transylvanian'' Prayer Rug, possibly late 19th century copy of a 17th century model. Metropolitan Museum of Art, Bequest of Joseph V. McMullan, 1973, 1974.149.13.

indicates that the original identification had been forgotten.

Still another change was the lamp's transformation into a ewer (ibriq), the implement used for ritual ablution before the start of the prayer. The ibriq could be either suspended or combined with other decorative features making it a vestigial lamp or an ornament (Figs. 11, 19, nos. XVII, XVIII). As to the choice of the ewer, one should here recall the passage in Ibn Battuta's *Voyages*, according to which the postulant brought only a sajjada and an ibriq with him when he entered the zawiya. One of the curious aspects of the ewer in the prayer carpet is the fact that it is nearly always hung upside down. This might indicate that it has already been used and is now empty.

Combining the niche with its mirror image at the opposite end as a kind of "counter-niche" introduced an entirely different approach to the basic setting of the prayer carpet. This was done according to the law of symmetry so frequently applied in carpet designs. It happened particularly in the "Transylvanian" and Ushak prayer carpets of the 17th century. Though the situation was now more complex, the worshiper was at first still aware of the proper arch to face during prayer, since only one arch showed the lamp. But, again, the law of symmetry was bound to take over and a lamp was inserted in the apex of both the opposing arches (Fig. 12). Though the design was now aesthetically pleasing, the original concept was obviously forgotten. Eventually the lamp motif was altogether deleted.

The development did not stop with the duplication of the niche. The arch design on the two sides of the field resembled the common compositional theme of the medallion rug, which not only has a central medallion, but also quarter medallions in the corners. Since the spandrels of the two opposing arches created a configuration similar to the two quarter medallions, it was natural that the double-arched prayer carpet eventually received a central medallion (Fig. 13). Even at this stage the weaver was aware of the original concept in spite of the central medallion and the second, or counter, niche, because it was at first only the original mihrab arch which received the lamp (Fig. 14). But soon there would be a lamp in both arches or substitute lamps. Another development consisted of adding a medallion to single arch compositions (no. IX), or even *two* medallions (no. XXXIV).

Occasionally decorative features connected the apexes of the two opposing arches with the central medallion. These were the echoes of the lamps, or rather of the chains, from which the lamps were suspended. Soon even this memory faded and the decorative "chains" were connected only with the central medallion like the shields and escutcheons which were often attached to the large central unit. Here the law of multiplication once again became active. Analagous to the multiple lamps, multiple decorative features, "suspended from chains," were connected with the central medallion.

Another basic compositional scheme filled the ground below the arch with flowers. Such a floral arrangement occurred in Persian and Ottoman prayer carpets of the 16th century (nos. I, II, IV & XXVI), and in those from Mughal India (Figs. 22, 23, nos. XXIII, XXIV) of the next century. The floral designs in these carpets were, however, differently rendered. The principal notion remained even though the floral forms were greatly reduced. They could have, for instance, been given the form of a central floral ribbon or of triple bands as in the case of the fields of Gördes (Ghiordes) and Kula carpets (Fig. 15). Since the design of Persian and Turkish carpets from the sixteenth century on is persistingly floral, the underlying concept has, generally speaking, nothing to do with the tree of life motif which is so

Figure 13—"Transylvanian" Prayer Rug, Anatolia, 17th-18th century. Metropolitan Museum of Art, Bequest of Joseph V. McMullan, 1973, 1974.149.15.

Figure 14—Prayer Rug, Anatolia, Ushak, 17th century. Metropolitan Museum of Art, Bequest of Joseph V. McMullan, 1973, 1974.149.11.

Figure 15—Prayer Rug, Anatolia, Kula, 19th century. Metropolitan Museum of Art, Gift of James F. Ballard, 22.100.80.

Figure 16—Prayer Rug, Anatolia, dated 1182 A.H. / A.D. 1768, possibly a later copy. Metropolitan Museum of Art, Bequest of Joseph V. McMullan, 1973, 1974.149.20.

22

common in Near Eastern art. Though this motif occasionally occurs in carpets (no. XLII) and printed wall hangings with an arched composition, the creative impulse seems to have been provided by the idea of the "garden," terrestrial or, more likely, celestial, since there are many Persian carpets of the 16th century which imply a paradisical setting by their inclusion of winged, angel-like creatures.

Being provided with a second major theme in the form of floral motifs, the possibilities of a creative rearrangement of themes and design units further proliferated. Very soon the lamp in a field of floral ornaments became a flower vase near the apex of the arch (nos. XIV and XV). Other solutions were that there was just a flower suspended instead of a vase or that the flower was placed in the general location without being actually fastened (no. XV). There was, however, no reason why such a container of flowers should be connected with the arch as such. It was therefore moved to the bottom of the field, where it then looked as if the whole flowery arrangement emanated from it (no. XXVII).

How the increase of constituent ideas enriched the visual aspect of the prayer rugs by way of a cross-fertilization of motifs can be deduced from a group of carpets in which the elements lamp, medallion and flower were made to interact in a novel fashion. Such a development is suggested by the strange central unit in an Ottoman prayer rug in the Textile Museum (no. III). Here the elongated medallion has a finial on one side only and the growth of the inserted flowers distinguishes it from the usual symmetrical and two-sided arrangement of these central units (Figs. 13, 14, nos. VIII and IX). It may very well be that this shape was inspired by the pointed area delineated by the suspension chains of the lamp just above it. They, too, mark an area ending in a point whose lower form is, however, so-to-say truncated by the suspended lamp. An awareness of this space is indicated by the fact that in a number of prayer rugs the space between the chains has been set off by a color which is different from that of the surrounding field and in a few cases even by an inserted decorative design. Subsequently this marked space assumed a life of its own and this in disregard of its generic premises. By having its form completed at its lower end it turned into a full-fledged medallion; this was then filled with flowers for decoration, but also for a continued stressing of the vertical direction. Finally the newly developed unit was, like all medallions, moved toward the center of the rug (see also no. XI). All these changes meant the arrival of a new, independent element within the concept of the prayer rug.

There are additional themes of lesser importance which played a role in the ever-changing compositional schemes. For instance, the outlines of the feet at the lower end of the sajjada marked the appropriate place to stand for prayer. Though the intent of this feature is obvious, it was, nevertheless, altered by giving the appropriate shapes a more general form (Fig. 9) and by eventually turning them into a flower-like ornament (no. XXII). Devoid of meaning, the motif was moved higher up in the field thereby attaining a more conspicuous place in the decoration of the carpet; or it was placed wherever the aesthetic requirements of the composition demanded it (nos. IX and XXII) and sometimes provisions were even unknowingly made for three or four feet (nos. XXXIV and XL).

The columns at the side of the field were another element which went from functional significance to decorative embellishment. Originally these columns had the tectonic purpose of supporting the weight of the crowning arch. This can be seen particularly in the properly executed columns which have an implied sense of roundness, and appropriate bases and capitals (no. I). Indeed, there still exist, as shown in an article by May H. Beattie, several 17th and 18th century examples which display either two architecturally executed columns at either side of a single arch (no. V) or six columns to support a triple arcade (nos. XII & XIII). In this tripartite composition there may well be a faint echo of the arrangement of the Roman Triumphal Arch or, more specifically, of the occasional triple sequence of mihrabs. What is more significant is the fact that an awareness of architectural necessities persisted in a good many examples. However, even the early design of columns in Turkish carpets was influenced, not by architectural functions but by decorative requirements; hence, the columns are overlaid with unrelated patterns (no. XIV). This is consistent with the debilitating effects of decorative tendencies in other Anatolian carpets of the late 17th and 18th century. This mixing of diverse elements is not, however, an exclusively Turkish feature as shown by a splendid Mughal-Indian sajjada in the Museum of Decorative Arts in Vienna whose polylobed arch is supported at each side by a half-cypress rising from a container-like base and met on top by a half-floral pendant (p. 133, Fig. 24; see also no. XXVII).

The predilection to ornamentation led to the final destruction of the architectural aspect of the column within the composition. In the course of the 18th century, the columns increasingly bore ornamental patterns from which occasionally little flowers sprouted in parallel lines. Thus the columns have the appearance of flat, ornamental ribbons. The untectonic nature of these elements which once had been columns becomes evident from a whole series of inappropriate features: the "column" has a flower instead of a capital and is no longer connected with the arch it is supposed to support (Fig. 11 and no. XIV); or conversely, the "column" ends in a triangular tip which rests on a flower instead of a base (no. XVII). Two versions present perhaps the most telling indications of this non-tectonic development. In one, the columns are placed on water ewers shown upside down (Fig. 10). This combination, though physically impossible, was apparently mentally and emotionally satisfactory to the Muslim user as the design remains within the proper range of mental associations. In the second case the weaver reached a logical conclusion and dispensed with the columns altogether by combining the triple arch with its mirror image on the other side of the field. At first, he still kept the capitals of the opposing arcades (Fig. 16), though he did eventually dispense with these last vestiges of the original supports. In this procedure the monochrome triple field, which in the basic design was the open space or void within the arcade (and therefore represented a negative aspect, nos. XII, XIII and XIX), took on a positive role and appeared as a major, ribbon-like feature which was occasionally decorated with rosettes or other ornamental designs.

Though the concept of the direction-giving mihrab-like arch was greatly weakened when the arch was duplicated in mirror fashion on the other side of the field, there was an even more pronounced way in which this basic feature of the sajjada was negated. In one of the earliest preserved prayer carpets (although to judge from its "baroque" aspect, probably a later development of the type), a piece in the Museum of East Berlin and generally attributed to Egypt and the early 16th century, there is, in the field formed by the arch, an octagonal area which is open and has a short connection with the inner guard stripe (p. 130, Fig. 19). In other examples from Anatolia, this connecting link becomes longer and narrower, but the basic octagonal outline of the form persists regardless of which form the crowning arch takes: polylobed, triangular, or in some cases, octagonal (or even heptagonal) (nos. VIII & IX). This strange element has been interpreted by Johanna Zick as a smaller mihrab niche within the larger one, just as this feature occurs in actual mihrabs of Persian and Anatolian mosques of the 13th to the 15th centuries (Fig. 17). More recently Volkmar Enderlein has pointed out that the discrepancy of the larger and lower "niche" is too strong and he has therefore suggested that the design represents a water basin with a feeding water course similar to the ones shown in Persian miniatures of the 15th century and later on. He supported this hypothesis by pointing to the existence of such water basins for ablution purposes in mosques as well as to the inclusion of a ewer in the field of the early Cairene rug (Fig.19). It may well be that both interpretations are correct. The early inclusion of the ewer close to the octagonal area and the great differences of the outlines in the two "niches" in the sajjada in Berlin make the interpretation of a water basin the more likely as representing the original concept. However, once the upper niche was given a polygonal shape which, to judge from a painting of St. Ursula by Carpaccio, occurred before the end of the 15th century, the similarly shaped lower unit could very well have been interpreted as a second niche (see also nos. XXXIV-XXXVII). This was certainly so at the later stages of the development. It happened, when for reasons of harmony, the octagonal units were made to give up their "one way" direction and became mirror images of each other. But, while it was the "counter niche" in the "Transylvanian" group which reflected the main niche, it is here the main niche which adapts itself to the bottom niche by reversing its direction. From a carpet in the Ballard Collection in St. Louis, it is evident that the weaver considered both these designs as "mihrabs," since lamplike appendices are suspended from both polygonal units. The overall effect is so unlike that of the usual sajjada that in the catalogue the carpet was not placed in this category. Of course, others without any hanging lamps in the confronting niches are even less recognizable from what they had originally been.

In conclusion: in surveying both the general composition of the sajjada, especially in Anatolia, and its individual motifs one is constantly reminded of the weakening of the original symbolism, especially in the 18th century. The basic design was at times invaded by associative motifs, but more commonly fell prey to a strong decorative tendency which elaborated the original composition, but in doing so weakened, if not destroyed, the primary concept. Both the proliferation of small patterns and the urge to create symmetrical compositions were the forces which transfigured the archetypes. Surprisingly through this process of "beautification" and "harmonization," the newly created versions remained attractive to the customers, especially the uninitiated ones, and the revamped traditions often lasted longer in an appreciative ambiance than in the case of other classical types. The final reason for these transformations and their ready acceptance by a large clientele may well be that an initial reflection of three-dimensional architecture had at last been changed into forms appropriate to the textile arts. They therefore satisfied instinctive aesthetic attitudes more readily.

*This paper reproduces a lecture, only slightly enlarged, which was given by the writer to the Hajji Baba Club of New York on December 8th, 1971. Besides the illustrations accompanying this essay, the reader should consider the pertinent prayer rugs of the exhibition which are referred to by their given Roman numerals.

TURKISH
PRAYER RUGS

Some of the earliest prayer rugs of Turkey go back to the fifteenth century and are based to a great extent on traditions of Seljuk art. Three important early examples are in the Museum of Turkish and Islamic Art of Istanbul, and belong to the category of multiple or mosque prayer rugs (saff). One of these rugs, in fragmentary condition, has two prayer niches left in blue on white ground, with three mosque lamps hanging from the apex and the sides of the arch. A similar rug is hanging over a balustrade in a fresco in Palazzo Scrofa Calcagnini, in Ferrara, by the Italian painter, Ercole Grandi (1463-1525). The second rug, also a fragment of a multiple prayer rug, has two purple panels, separated by yellow bands, and decorated with geometrical design based on Kufic letters and hook motifs. The third rug, probably the latest of the group, has two rows of eight angular prayer niches on a dark blue ground. The red border has Kufic writing, with letters ending in half palmettes. Such borders are identical to those in a number of "Holbein" and "Lotto" rugs of the fifteenth and sixteenth centuries, attributed to the looms of Anatolia.

Ottoman court prayer rugs can be dated to the end of the sixteenth and early seventeenth centuries, and should be regarded as products of Turkish court manufactories of Bursa and Istanbul. They are decorated with floral patterns, which are characteristic of Ottoman art of Turkey. These prayer rugs, together with larger rugs with similar floral patterns, were frequently regarded as products of Turkish court looms, by others as "Damascus." In recent years, it was suggested by the German scholar, Kurt Erdmann, and later by Ernst Kühnel, that these rugs, together with earlier rugs with geometrical patterns, were made on Cairo looms. Erdmann gradually changed his opinion regarding these prayer rugs and called some of them products of "Cairo or Istanbul," others of "Istanbul or Bursa." New evidence found in the Museum of Turkish and Islamic Art in Istanbul establishes definitely that most of these prayer rugs were products of Istanbul court looms. A rug from the mosque of Sultan Ahmet (1617) in Istanbul is, according to a contemporary label, designated as "Istanbul isi" — "made in Istanbul." This rug is related to the column prayer rugs described below.

There are two main types of Ottoman prayer rugs of court manufacture. In one of them, the field with a niche has a candelabra composition of various composite palmettes with curling lanceolate leaves and sprays of plum blossoms (Vienna Museum, Walters Art Gallery and McMullan Collection). The other type has a plain field with slender columns supporting the arch of the niche (Metropolitan Museum; Berlin Museum; Museum of Turkish and Islamic Art, Istanbul). The border decoration of these rugs is floral and consists of palmettes, pomegranates, carnations, hyacinths, tulips, roses and lanceolate leaves, ornaments well known from the decoration of Ottoman mosques from the end of the sixteenth and early seventeenth centuries. One of the prayer rugs in the Berlin Museum is dated 1610-11. A unique Ottoman prayer rug in the Textile Museum of Washington has a Hebrew inscription, which indicates that it was made for a synagogue. The Turkish character of the Ottoman decoration reveals that it must have been made in Istanbul in the beginning of the seventeenth century.

In court prayer rugs of the middle and second half of the seventeenth century, the texture coarsens and the design becomes stereotyped. The number of Senna (Senneh) knots per square inch is as low as ninety.

Related to sixteenth and seventeenth century Ushaks with star-shaped or oval medallions are a number of prayer rugs. Most of the early examples have a small central medallion with a prayer niche at each end. Such rugs appear in European paintings from the middle of the sixteenth to the middle of the seventeenth century. The spandrels are decorated with arabesques or cloud bands and the borders show either cloud bands or floral motifs of palmettes combined with arabesques. Such borders are also known to us from "Lotto" rugs and other types of Ushak rugs. The colors are usually deep: the fields are red, the borders blue or yellow, the spandrels blue, red or green.

The manufacture of prayer rugs of the Ushak type continued in the eighteenth century, but the floral scrolls are now geometrically stylized and the prayer niches are often disguised as narrow arched bands, forming the inner border of the field. In some of them, the arch is only at one end, usually the bottom end of the rug, while the top is in the form of a gable. Also, multiple prayer rugs of the Ushak type are known, in which the floral

Ottoman Court Rugs

Ushak Prayer Rugs

27

decoration of the larger medallion Ushaks is used in the field and the spandrels. A rug of this type is in the collection of Mr. and Mrs. Frank Michaelian and can be dated to the middle of the eighteenth century.

Bergama Prayer Rugs

The looms of Bergama (the ancient Pergamon) in Western Anatolia produced, since the sixteenth century, several types of Turkish rugs. Erdmann attributed to Bergama several sixteenth and seventeenth century types of geometrical rugs, including the so-called "Holbeins" with large octagons or lozenges within squares. This type of "Holbein" continued to be made during the eighteenth and nineteenth centuries.

The best known type of seventeenth century Bergama prayer rug, also known as Transylvanians, has either one niche or two at each end of the field. In most of them, one or two mosque lamps are placed in the apex of the niches and are connected by angular floral scrolls. The spandrels are decorated either with arabesques or floral motifs. The borders show a series of cartouches alternating with star-shaped compartments, both containing arabesques and floral scrolls. The characteristic features of these prayer rugs are the guard bands, which, in most cases, show a reciprocal design of trefoils. The design of these prayer rugs is rendered in vivid colors of red, blue, yellow and green. Bergama prayer rugs were popular in Europe and may be seen in some Dutch paintings of the seventeenth century — for example, in a famous portrait of Abraham Grapheus by Cornelis de Vos (1620), in the Royal Museum of Fine Arts at Antwerp. The eighteenth century examples of Bergama prayer rugs show variations of the earlier models. Instead of mosque lamps, we find a central compartment, usually a lozenge-shaped medallion, containing floral motifs. A well-known American portrait of Isaac Royall and his family, painted by Robert Feke in 1741, now in the Harvard Law Library, shows an eighteenth century type of Bergama, with large rosettes in the border combined with the cartouches of the earlier types.

Ladik Prayer Rugs

A group of prayer rugs was woven during the eighteenth and nineteenth centuries in the town and district of Ladik, the ancient Laodicea. The Ladiks have many peculiar features, which distinguish them from other types of Anatolian rugs. The early Ladiks, which can be dated to the first half of the eighteenth century, are known as column Ladiks. Their decoration consists of a triple arch supported by slender double columns. Such rugs are sometimes called Transylvanians, as they were frequently found in churches of Transylvania or Siebenbürgen, a province of Hungary. These early Ladiks have either a red or a white ground, while the borders have a series of lobed cartouches, filled with floral devices, chiefly tulips. Fine examples of these early Ladiks are in the Mc Mullan Collection and in the Ballard Collection of the St. Louis Museum. Above the niches of these Ladiks appear panels with arches shaped like arrowheads (sometimes called "Vandykes"), from which stalks issue ending in stylized lilies or tulips. In the later Ladiks, which can be dated to the second half of the eighteenth century, the panels with arches and stylized stalks of tulips appear above or below the niche. The borders of these later Ladiks, some of which bear dates, 1771, 1795 and 1799, have a decoration different from the column Ladiks. It consists of a series of composite rosettes alternating with stylized sprays of tulips. The field of these later Ladiks has usually a single arch with or without columns. In some of them, like the rug in the Metropolitan Museum of Art, dated 1795, two columns are placed in the center of the niche and are converted into decorative bands. The manufacture of Ladiks continued into the nineteenth century but the weavers frequently misunderstood the traditional design and transformed the floral motifs into semi-geometrical forms.

One of the largest known groups of Anatolian prayer rugs of the eighteenth and nineteenth centuries is that made by peasant weavers in the town and district of Ghiordes. The decoration of these prayer rugs is mostly floral and occurs in the borders and spandrels of the niche. Occasionally, the floral decoration fills the field as well. The flowers and fruits seen in Ghiordes rugs are those most favored by Ottoman artists, namely, carnations, hyacinths, tulips, lilies, roses and pomegranates. Adopting some of the floral patterns of the court rugs, the Ghiordes weavers stylized them gradually more and more. In early examples, probably of the middle and second half of the eighteenth century, the design of the borders closely follows that of the court prayer rugs with large palmettes and lanceolate leaves. Their niche usually rests upon two columns, which in later rugs become decorative pilasters or floral festoons. The mosque lamp in the niche is turned frequently into a vase or floral device, and the columns rest on ewers of a shape well known in nineteenth century Turkey. Most of the Ghiordes prayer rugs are of the nineteenth century and are decorated with floral, strongly stylized motifs, which appear in the borders, the spandrels and the guard bands. In some of the Ghiordes rugs, there are no columns or festoons. The field of the niche is plain and bordered by a row of small flowers, such as carnations. The Ghiordes prayer rugs have harmonious color compositions of red and blue, with the addition of white, yellow and other colors.

The Ghiordes weavers also produced two other distinctive types of prayer rugs: the Kis-Ghiordes, or betrothal rug, and the so-called cemetery rug. According to Turkish tradition, the Kis-Ghiordes rugs were woven by young women as part of their dowry. Their features include a niche at either end of the field with a jeweled ornament hanging from the apex of each arch. The decoration of the field and border consists usually of a series of small leaves. In the cemetery rugs, the field of the niche is decorated with rows of tombs and cypress trees and with other floral motifs.

Prayer rugs similar to those of Ghiordes were made in Kula not far from Ghiordes. The borders of the Kula prayer rugs are often divided into as many as eight or nine narrow stripes, decorated with rows of small blossoms. In most of the Kulas, yellows and blues predominate. The niche has an all over pattern of small floral motifs or there is a central festoon composed of minute lamps from which issue clusters of eight-pointed stars. Like Ghiordes, Kula was also known for cemetery prayer rugs, showing the characteristic multi-striped border.

To Melas, in Central Anatolia, is attributed a type of nineteenth century Turkish prayer rug, which in many ways is related to the Bergama group. The characteristic features of the Melas prayer rugs include an angular version of the horseshoe-arch and a floral border consisting of round blossoms and leaves, the latter often forming cross devices. Other small

Ghiordes (Gördes) and Kula Prayer Rugs

Melas and Mujur Prayer Rugs

Melas rugs have a geometrical pattern of octagons or star-shaped medallions. At one or both ends of these rugs, there is often a band with stylized palmettes or tulips.

To the looms of Mujur, also in Central Anatolia, are assigned nineteenth century prayer rugs with a niche showing a pointed arch and a transverse panel with a row of arches, recalling similar motifs of the Ladiks. In some of them, the niche contains a stylized tree, as seen on a rug of the Metropolitan Museum. The Mujur prayer rugs have a distinctive border, with rows of lozenges within squares, enclosing either stylized rosettes or star motifs.

Tapestry-Woven Prayer Rugs (Kilims) of Turkey

During the eighteenth and nineteenth centuries, peasant craftsmen of Anatolian villages made prayer rugs in tapestry technique, known as kilims. In some of them, metal threads are added. As with the pile rugs, regional differences may be detected in their design. They have usually one niche, although occasionally triple arched niches appear as in a kilim in the Metropolitan Museum of Art, with a floral design of stylized carnations. This kilim was probably made in the Ghiordes or Kula district. One of the kilims in the Metropolitan Museum of Art is dated 1774/75 A. D. and shows an affinity to Ladik prayer rugs.   M.S.D.

I

Ottoman Court Manufactory, Bursa (?), late 16th century

Loaned by The Metropolitan Museum of Art, Gift of James F. Ballard, 22.100.51

This outstanding prayer rug, probably the most famous in existence today, displays patterned columns supporting three arches with a mosque lamp hanging in the center. The favorite Turkish flowers of tulips and carnations are visible between the carefully rendered column bases. Split palmette leaves and small blossoms pattern the spandrels. In the horizontal panel above the spandrels, four domed buildings and varied flora appear between the curved crenelations. A prototype for the use of a horizontal panel exists on the earliest surviving prayer rug, a Mamluk rug woven in Cairo in about 1500 (p. 130, Fig. 19) (Enderlein, pp. 8 ff.; Zick, pp. 7, 14). A horizontal panel also appears on many later Anatolian prayer rugs (nos. XII-XIX). The exquisite clarity of the curvilinear drawing and the harmonious balance of motifs especially in the main border of this rug reveal the heights attained by the Ottoman court designers and weavers. The use of several delicate color tones (light blue in particular) further characterizes these court rugs.

The design scheme of this rug is one of the four types surviving among the Ottoman court prayer rugs which share the technical features of silk warps and wefts with Senneh knots in colored wool and white (and sometimes light blue) cotton. This use of silk warps and wefts produces an ex-

quisitely light and supple rug. The three other surviving types all have a single niche displaying one of several designs: an undecorated field with columns (p. 130, Fig. 20; Islamic Museum, East Berlin); an undecorated field without columns (fragment, Museum of Turkish and Islamic Art, Istanbul; Ellis 1969, fig. 2); and a profusely decorated floral and foliate field without columns (no. II, The Walters Art Gallery).

Size: L. 1.677m (5′6′′) × W. 1.27m (4′2′′).
Warp: silk, ivory, 2 I-yarns Z-plied and 2 I-yarns S-plied, alternate warps slightly depressed.
Weft: silk, red, I-yarns, 2 shots.
Pile: wool, 2 S-yarns; cotton (ivory and light blue), 2 Z-yarns; Senneh knot open on the left (slant to left), 18 horiz. × 16 vert. per in. (288 per sq. in.).
Color: 8, crimson, blue-green, dark blue, light blue, medium green, dark green, tan, ivory.
Condition: woven bottom end first, scattered areas of repair, especially in central niche, no original ends or selvedges.
Published: Dimand 1973, no. 105, fig. 188, color; Dickie, frontispiece; Ellis 1969, fig. 4; Beattie 1968, fig. 1; Schlosser, no. 14; Bode & Kühnel, fig. 53; Dilley, pl. XLVI, color; Dimand 1958, fig. 204; Breck & Morris, no. 24.

I

II
Ottoman Court Manufactory, Bursa (?), late 16th century
Loaned by The Walters Art Gallery, 81.4

The extraordinary field of this prayer rug contains no columns but displays a sophisticated pattern of beautifully rendered blossoms and leaves which are characteristic of all media of Ottoman court art (cf. p. 129, Figs. 17 & 18). The specific composition may in fact have been adapted from patterns on some large Ottoman court rugs (Ellis 1969, pp. 5, 6). The spandrels display a finely drawn arabesque which serves as a prototype for many later Turkish rugs. Scalloped quarter-medallions fill the lower corners of the niche and are patterned by an Ottoman court version of the Chinese cloud band.

Two rugs exist which are extremely similar to the Walters' rug. One, in Vienna, displays different combinations of delicate colors (Erdmann 1962, pl. VII, color); the other, in the McMullan collection, has noticeably stronger coloration and is technically dissimilar to the other two in its lack of any cotton in the pile (McMullan, pl. 4, color). The Vienna and Walters' rugs share the technical features of silk warps and wefts with Senneh knots in colored wool and white and light blue cotton. Among the few prayer rugs in this technique, all except the Walters' rug have the same main border and guard stripe patterns as the Metropolitan's rug, no. I. The Walters' main border pattern displays medallions with Turkish flowers, tulips and hyacinths, alternating with cloud bands and lotus-bearing vines. Several

stylistic features of this rug also occur on a large and very fine but technically dissimilar all-wool rug in the Metropolitan Museum of Art (Dimand 1973, fig. 184, color detail). These include the patterns of both the main border and the guard stripe, the shape and drawing of the corner medallions, and much of the field pattern. The strong, rich colors of the large Metropolitan rug appear very similar to those on the McMullan prayer rug. These last two rugs may tentatively be ascribed to a different court manufactory in the Istanbul area.

Analysis courtesy of Charles Grant Ellis.
Size: L. 1.803m (5'11") × W. 1.257m (4' 1½").
Warp: silk, yellow, 2 Z-yarns S-plied, warps on 2 levels.
Weft: silk, red, I-yarns, 2 shots.
Pile: wool, 3 S-yarns; cotton (ivory and light blue), 3 Z-yarns, Senneh knot open on the left, 19 horiz. × 20 vert. per in. (380 per sq. in.).
Color: 9, wine-red, dark blue, light blue, blue-green, light green, yellow, greenish-yellow, "ex-orange," ivory.
Condition: considerable reknotting along central axis of rug, in spandrels, upper and lower parts of field, outer guard stripes at sides, no original ends or selvedges.
Published: Dimand 1973, fig. 187; Ellis 1969, fig. 6; Erdmann 1961, Abb. 15; *Bulletin of Art Institute of Chicago,* XLI, no. 2, pl. 18.

III
Ottoman Design, Cairo,
mid-17th century
The Textile Museum, 1967.24.1

Although this all-wool rug was designed by Ottoman court artists, both stylistic and technical features suggest that it was not woven on the court looms which produced nos. I and II, or the McMullan prayer rug discussed under no. II. The scale and outline of the wine-red niche maintain the handsome proportions seen in the Walters' rug (no. II); however, the green arabesque in the spandrels is less precisely rendered and a red and yellow checkerboard pattern has been added. Two new features not found in the few Ottoman court manufactory prayer rugs with silk warp and weft are the shape of the corner medallions and the central bouquet of typically Ottoman flowers. One other all-wool rug, believed to be "the prayer rug of Sultan Ahmet I" in the Topkapi Saray, Istanbul, is similar but has a far more gracefully drawn central bouquet (Ettinghausen 1966, p. 214, color). The addition on the Textile Museum rug of the mosque lamp hanging on three chains from the lower edge of the main border is awkward and crowds the field (cf. p. 129, Figs. 17 & 18). While the guard stripes are similar to those found on the imperial silk warp and weft rugs, the main border with its pattern of lotus blossoms and lanceolate leaves is more characteristic of the all-wool rugs of this quality. This main border pattern successfully fills the side borders and the four corners. The bottom and top borders, however, display a spacing problem in the center which altered the natural continuity of the pattern. A similar occurrence appears on no. IV. The exact provenance of these all-wool rugs of non-court quality has been disputed. Recently they were reattributed to the environs of Istanbul (Dimand 1973, pp. 196 ff.). They are, however, generally accepted as having been made in Cairo, which the Ottomans conquered in 1517. Designs were supplied by the Ottoman court artists in Istanbul for use by the Cairene artisans in a variety of media including rugs (Kühnel 1957, pp. 41 ff.; Ellis 1969, p. 13). It should be noted that this particular rug is said to have been found in "a mosque in southern Spain" (American Art Association, *The V. and L. Benguiat Private Collection of Rare Old Rugs*, Sale Dec. 4,5, 1925, New York, no. 45).

Size: L. 1.83m (6') × W. 1.27m (4'2'').
Warp: wool, pale yellow, 4 S-yarns Z-plied, alternate warps depressed.
Weft: wool, pale red, 2-4 S-yarns, 3 shots.
Pile: wool, 2 S-yarns and 3 S-yarns, Senneh knot open on the left (slant to left), 12 horiz. × 12 vert. per in. (144 per sq. in.).
Color: 6, wine-red, medium green, medium blue, yellow, ivory, dark brown.
Condition: woven bottom end first, dark brown forming ground of main border mostly disintegrated, borders worn, no original ends or selvedges.
Published: Ellis 1969, fig. 13; American Art Association, *The V. and L. Benguiat Private Collection of Rare Old Rugs*, Sale Dec. 4,5, 1925, New York, no. 45.

III

IV
Ottoman Design, Cairo,
mid or late 17th century

Loaned by The Metropolitan Museum of Art, Bequest of Isaac D. Fletcher, 17.120.137

Although this rug is stylistically related to the Walters' rug (no. II), close examination reveals many differences. The leaves and blossoms on the wine-red ground are less clearly drawn on this rug and are encumbered by the large round blossom in the center of the field, a feature which suggests the composition's dependence on larger rugs. The broader proportions of the niche are less graceful than on the Walters' rug and quatre-foil corner medallions instead of scalloped medallions appear at the bottom of the field. The unusual main border decoration is composed of favorite Turkish flowers, with large tulips filling the four corners. The spacing of this floral pattern at the bottom and top of the rug is faulty and results in an awkward repetition of the carnation and pomegranate motifs in the center of the border. This, together with the other features, suggests that the rug was not woven in one of the best workshops. Instead of having a silk foundation and white and blue cotton in the pile as in the Walters' rug, this and several other very similar rugs of non-court quality are all-wool and are considerably more loosely woven (Ellis 1969, figs. 15-18). Although displaying an Ottoman court design, the exact provenance of these all-wool rugs

remains unresolved. Evidence suggests they are probably from the rug-weaving center of Cairo which the Ottomans conquered in 1517 (Kühnel 1957, pp. 41 ff.), although some authors believe they are from the environs of Istanbul (Dimand 1973, pp. 196 ff.).

Size: L. 1.65m (5'5'') × W. 1.18m, top (3'10½''), 1.27m, bottom (4'2'').
Warp: wool, ivory, 4 S-yarns Z-plied, alternate warps depressed, ends dyed light green.
Weft: wool, red (some yellow), 3 S-yarns, 2 and 3 shots.
Pile: wool, 2 S, 3 S and 4 S-yarns, Senneh knot open on the left, 11 horiz. × 11 vert. per in. (121 per sq. in.).
Color: 7, red, medium blue, yellow, forest green, light green, ivory, brown-black.
Condition: worn areas with scattered repair, the original brown-black ground of main border disintegrated and replaced by varying shades of green, no original ends, fragmentary 2 cord selvedge.
Published: Dimand 1973, cat. no. 108, fig. 191; Ellis 1969, fig. 14; Erdmann 1961, Abb. 6.

38

IV

V
Synagogue Rug, Cairo, early 17th century
The Textile Museum, R 16.4.4 (R1.62)

While the general appearance of this rug displays certain similarities with the Ottoman-designed prayer rugs, two features without any known parallels are immediately apparent: the large cup in which nine lamps are suspended and the Hebrew inscription which reads, "This is the Gate of the Lord through which the righteous enter," Psalm 118, verse 20. Certain irregularities occur in the form and spacing of the letters which indicate that the rug probably was not woven by someone literate in the Hebrew language. However, a Jew of strict observance must have copied the text from Psalms since the word for God has been piously abbreviated for this less sacred location on a rug. The small dome at the top which interrupts the main border pattern in an extraordinary manner may further suggest the "Gate of the Lord" (Kühnel 1957, pp. 53-54). This is the only rug known of this period with an inscription in the horizontal panel above the spandrels. On some later Turkish rugs, pseudo-Arabic appears in two separate cartouches as on this rug, which suggests that an Ottoman court model may once have existed (cf. p. 129, Fig. 18). The representation of the large cup with lamps may be associated with an old Jewish tradition of donating glass lamps to synagogues. An Islamic prototype is not known.

Several stylistic features of this all-wool rug are closely comparable with those of the Metropolitan rug, no. I: the bases and capitals of the patterned columns; the presence of an array of blossoms between the column bases; and the pattern of the guard stripe. This popular guard stripe pattern also appears on the Textile Museum rug, no. III, where it flanks a main border with the same pattern. This main border pattern is characteristic of the quality of all-wool rugs traditionally attributed to Cairene manufacture (Ellis 1969, pp. 14, 15).

Size: L. 1.86m (6'1'') × W. 1.55m (5'1'').
Warp: wool, pale green, 4 S-yarns Z-plied, alternate warps very depressed.
Weft: wool, red, 3 S-yarns, 2 shots.
Pile: wool, 2 and 3 S-yarns, also 1 S and 1 Z-yarns, and 2 S and 1 Z-yarns, Senneh knot open on the left, 11.5 horiz. × 12 vert. per in. (138 per sq. in.).
Color: 8, crimson, emerald green, yellow-green, royal blue, light blue, yellow, tan, dark brown almost totally disintegrated.
Condition: woven bottom end first, worn with scattered repairs, dark brown disintegrated, 1 end: remnant, red wool, weft-faced plain weave; selvedges: remnant of 2 cords of 3 yellow warps.
Published: Cammann, p. 17, illus.; Ellis 1969, p. 14, illus. fig. 19; Beattie 1968, pp. 243 ff., illus. fig. 2; Dilley 1959, pl. XLIII; Kühnel 1957, pp. 53-54, pl. XXX, color.

V

VI
Multiple-Niche Prayer Rug Fragment or Saff, Cairo, late 17th century

Loaned by the Field Museum of Natural History, Chicago, 76940

Multiple-niche prayer rugs made in Egypt with as many as 132 mihrabs or as few as 10 mihrabs are recorded in a 1674 inventory of the Yeni Mosque in Istanbul which was completed under imperial directive during the reign of Sultan Mehmet IV (Sakisian, pp. 368, 370-371).

Due to its fragmentary condition, the original size of this rare and very worn Egyptian *saff* cannot be determined. Careful observation reveals the existence of at least twelve niches, composed of a minimum of three rows with four niches each. Only eight of the niches survive. Two additional niches appear to be from the only other comparable rug known (Field Museum of Natural History, Chicago). Several features are reminiscent of the designs on Ottoman court prayer rugs: the outline of the niche; the arabesques in the spandrels; the chevron patterned columns; and the undecorated field with a mosque lamp suspended by chains. The fields of the surviving niches are in five different colors: red, dark blue, emerald green, brown, and mustard. A narrow border, composed of the alternation of large and small blossoms on continuous stems, separates the niches and also serves as the main border, a fact which is confirmed by surviving selvedges. (The proportions of the rug

necessitated weaving the pattern sideways on the loom.) The loose weaving, the unrefined drawing, the compressed proportions of the niches, in addition to the unusual variations in the width of the niches, together suggest poor supervision and a late 17th century date. Except for the white cotton used in the pile, the technique and palette are characteristic of Ottoman Cairene rugs.

Reconstructed minimum size: L. 4.35m (14′3″) (warp) × W. 3.07m (10′1″) (weft).

Warp: wool, yellow and very pale red combined, 4 S-yarns Z-plied.

Weft: wool, grouped areas of yellow and red, yellow, red, 5 S-yarns, 2 shots.

Pile: wool, 3 and 4 S-yarns (polychrome); cotton, 2 Z-yarns (ivory), Senneh knot open on the left, 9 horiz. × 8 vert. per in. (72 per sq. in.).

Color: 9, royal blue, emerald green, light green, crimson, yellow, tan, brown, dark brown, ivory.

Condition: fragmentary, extremely worn, very little pile remains, no original ends, 1 selvedge: wool, 2 cords of multiple warps, attached by ground wefts around both cords.

Published: Ellis 1969, p. 16, not illus.

VII

Multiple-Niche Prayer Rug Fragment or Saff, Central Anatolia, late 16th-17th century

The Textile Museum, R 34.00.2

Probably the oldest surviving Anatolian *saff* in Western collections, this rug is also the only example known with this particular design. These factors plus the vibrant colors and bold drawing in the fragment far outweigh its imperfect appearance. On alternating ground colors of red and sapphire blue, a suspended mosque lamp bearing several motifs is flanked by two eight-pointed stars. The octagon and corner brackets, whose outlines vary in each niche, are closely comparable to designs on contemporary large-pattern "Holbein" rugs (e.g., Erdmann 1962, pl. 36; Dimand 1973, fig. 155). The handling of the arch of the niche is noteworthy with multiple bands outlining a handsomely proportioned stepped niche. The spandrels also display an unusual treatment; several bands form large triangles which contain variously colored corner brackets. The border pattern displays a lotus vine similar to those found on large-pattern "Holbein" rugs (e.g., Erdmann 1962, pl. 35) and some later rugs (no. XII). The combination of the various

motifs, the clarity of their drawing, and the brilliant colors, all suggest a relatively early date for this rug. Due to their proportions, *saffs* are usually woven with the design sideways on the loom so that the warps run parallel to the longer dimension (p. 136, Fig. 29).

Size: L. 1.74m (5' 8½'') (warp) × W. 1.47m (4' 10'') (weft).
Warp: wool, ivory, 2 Z-yarns S-plied.
Weft: wool, red, Z-yarns, 2 shots, lazy lines.
Pile: wool, 2 Z-yarns, Gördes knot (slant to left), 7 horiz. × 10 vert. per in. (70 per sq. in.).
Color: 8, red, wine-red, sapphire blue, medium blue, blue-green, yellow, dark brown, ivory.
Condition: heavily repaired with patches from rest of rug and Textile Museum small-pattern "Holbein" (R 34.17.1), very worn, spotted, cut down on all sides.
Published: Mackie, no. 29, illus.; Ellis 1963, fig. 19.

VIII
West or Central Anatolia, 16th-17th century

Loaned by The Metropolitan Museum of Art, Gift of James F. Ballard, 22.100.109

In contrast to most Anatolian prayer rugs which show a strong stylistic dependence on the Ottoman court-designed 16th century rugs, one group, exemplified by this rug and no. IX, appears to be part of a separate and not yet identifiable tradition. These rugs have several distinguishing features: the outline of the sides and bottom of the niche is not contiguous with the rug's border but is contained within the rectangular field of the rug; the arch is triangular; an undecorated vertical panel terminating in an octagon rises from the bottom center of the niche's outline; little if any decoration appears in the spandrels; and a few isolated floral elements decorate the niche's field. Johanna Zick suggests in her publication of this group of rugs that the vertical panel and octagon serve as a niche within a niche (Zick, p.7). Volkmar Enderlein offers what may be a more plausible explanation of this motif. He believes that a typically Islamic bird's-eye-view representation of a canal and water basin is shown. He associates their representation on a prayer rug with the ablutions performed before prayer and notes that a similar water basin surmounted by a depiction of a ewer appears on the oldest known prayer rug, the Mamluk (p.130, Fig. 19) (Enderlein, p.9).

The sides and lower border of the niche are outlined by a stylized running vine pattern; the arch of the niche has a narrower zigzag band. A degenerate version of this combination appears on some much later and otherwise unrelated Anatolian rugs (Dimand 1935, pl. XLIII). The main border pattern displays one of the most frequent patterns seen on these rugs, one in which large stylized palmettes on an angular scroll alternate with square units formed by terminating stems. Zick's extensive documentation of these rugs in European paintings is discussed under no. IX.

[In my view, the figure at the base of the field probably represents a mountain in a stylized form, such as may be seen at the bottom of Chinese dragon robes and temple pillar rugs. The worshiper thus stands upon elevated ground. C. G. Ellis]

Size: L. 1.755m (5′9′′) × W. 1.065m (3′6′′).
Warp: wool, ivory, 2 Z-yarns S-plied.
Weft: wool, light red, Z-yarns, 2 shots, lazy lines.
Pile: wool, 2 Z-yarns, Gördes knot, 9.5 horiz. × 12 vert. per in. (114 per sq. in.).
Color: 7, red, royal blue, blue-green, yellow, tan, brown-black, ivory.
Condition: woven bottom end first, some reweaving in central star-medallion, brown-black ground of inner guard mostly disintegrated, outer guard partially missing on 3 sides and completely missing at the top, no original ends or selvedges.
Published: Dimand 1973, cat. no. 80, illus.; Breck & Morris, no. 28, illus.

46

VIII

IX
West or Central Anatolia, 18th century
Loaned by The Metropolitan Museum of Art, Gift of James F. Ballard, 22.100.114

Although this rug is closely related to no. VIII, certain differences are immediately apparent. The more compressed proportions of this example, the decorated stripe outlining the niche and enlarged canal and water basin, the two large triangles bearing angular vines and leaves, and the incomplete main border pattern are all features of the design of this later rug. While this type of central medallion pattern is perhaps less frequently represented than that seen on no. VIII, the two symmetrically drawn foliate motifs above it are very common. The two large triangles are adopted from regular, non-prayer, rugs in which four large triangles square off the central medallion (e.g., The Textile Museum, nos. 8, 23; McMullan, pl. 100). The pattern which fills the niche's outline stripe and that of the main border are both seen on an Anatolian rug in the McMullan collection (McMullan, pl. 75). Insufficient space for the large scale of the main border pattern has caused it to be severely cropped at the top of its design.

Few representations of Turkish prayer rugs occur among the many Turkish rugs depicted by European artists in their paintings. However, extensive research by Zick has yielded numerous representations of rugs of this group by Italian artists dating from 1469 through 1562 (Zick, pp. 11

ff.). Although the style of no. VIII is closely comparable to that of a rug in an Italian painting of *ca.* 1519, it cannot be ascertained whether the rug could be that early. Details of no. IX, the compressed proportions and the lack of design clarity, suggest that it is a considerably later version of the original 16th century designs.

[This rug shows what is likely to have been the older form of the motif, as discussed under no. VIII, although the rug itself may be younger. C.G. Ellis]

Size: L. 1.525m (5') × W. 1.195m (3'11'').
Warp: wool, ivory, 2 Z-yarns S-plied.
Weft: wool, light red, Z-yarns, 2 shots, no lazy lines.
Pile: wool, 2 Z-yarns, Gördes knot, 7 horiz. × 11 vert. per in. (77 per sq. in.).
Color: 7, red, medium blue, light blue, medium green, mustard, brown-black, ivory.
Condition: woven bottom end first, rewoven areas in border, brown-black ground of main border mostly disintegrated, no original ends or selvedges.
Published: Dimand 1973, cat. no. 79, illus.; Breck & Morris, no. 29, illus.

IX

X
Ushak, first half 17th century
Loaned by The Metropolitan Museum of Art, Gift of James F. Ballard, 22.100.113

The field of this rug displays a very rare feature in that its pattern is composed of three rows of a design which frequently fills the borders of 16th and 17th century Ushak rugs. The design serves also as the main border of this rug. The arrangement of palmettes flanked by the leaves of an arabesque is directional, a fact the rug's designer took into account in planning the main border where the direction of the design is altered to face inward on each side. The same design, however, faces only one direction in the field, except in the right spandrel.

This rug stands apart from most Turkish prayer rugs which emphasize the arch and display differing motifs in the field and spandrels. The departure from these usual features and particularly the use of a border pattern to form the field suggest that this rug was not a product of one of the major rug manufactories in Ushak. Both the border design and coloring, however, can be compared to the large medallion, star, and alternate-star patterns attributed to Ushak, a city

recorded as early as the 16th century as a rug-weaving center (Bode & Kühnel, p. 39).

A slightly larger rug in the McMullan collection features a similar adoption of this border pattern for the field; however, a balanced layout is achieved by reversing the direction of alternate rows (McMullan, pl. 79, color).

Size: L. 1.525m (5') × W. 1.04m (3'5'').
Warp: wool, ivory, 2 Z-yarns S-plied, alternate warps slightly depressed.
Weft: wool, red, Z-yarns, 2 shots, lazy lines.
Pile: wool, 2 Z-yarns, Gördes knot (slight slant to left), 11 horiz. × 13.5 vert. per in. (150 per sq. in.).
Color: 7, red, salmon, yellow, brown, deep blue, medium blue, ivory.
Condition: woven bottom end first, reknotting along central axis and upper right, new bottom outer guard, no original ends or selvedges.
Published: Dimand 1973, no. 84, fig. 170; Breck & Morris, no. 31, illus.

X

XI
Multiple-Niche Prayer Rug or Saff, Ushak, 17th-early 18th century
Loaned by Mrs. Frank M. Michaelian

The size, condition and age of this rug and the rarity of its pattern all contribute to its importance among Turkish rugs. The same pattern and color scheme appear in each of the twelve niches. The surprisingly curvilinear nature of the drawing plus the individual motifs and their location are aspects of the design which closely reflect the earlier Ottoman court art (cf. p. 129, Figs. 17 & 18), especially the rugs attributed to Bursa and to Cairene looms. The placement and drawing of the suspended mosque lamp with the floral medallion beneath and the presence of arabesques in the spandrels can all be seen on the earlier Textile Museum rug, no. III. The prototype, however, for the large monochrome ivory blossoms which cover the red ground of each niche is more elusive and may have developed from an unknown, simpler version of the foliation on the Walters' rug, no. II (Ellis 1969, p. 17). A large fragment with this same pattern is also known (Museum of Turkish and Islamic Art, Istanbul, no. 776; Anon. 1961, pl. 5, color; Ellis 1969, fig. 24; Erdmann 1970, fig. 127).

Three other rugs, two large fragments and one large *saff*, can be cited which share the same layout and general coloring but have two stylistic variations resulting from the use of different Ottoman court prototypes. Instead of arabesques, the span-

drel decoration is a floral branch as seen on the East Berlin rug (p. 130, Fig. 20), and polychrome instead of monochrome flowering branches fill the field (Ellis 1969, figs. 21-23, color illus. of fig. 21: Anon. 1961, pl. 21). Several of these fragments were found in the Mosque of Sultan Selim in Edirne (Ellis 1969, p. 17).

The attribution of this group of *saffs* to Ushak, based on similarities with the large medallion and star-patterned rugs, is supported by a record indicating that *saffs* were made there. A 1674 inventory of the Yeni Mosque in Istanbul lists two *saffs* from Ushak (see no. VI; Sakisian, p. 371).

Size: L. 4.52m (14' 10'') (warp) × W. 2.995m (9' 10'') (weft).
Warp: wool, ivory, 2 Z-yarns S-plied, alternate warps depressed.
Weft: wool, pale red, Z-yarns, 2 shots.
Pile: wool, 2 Z-yarns, Gördes knot (slight slant to left), 8.5 horiz. × 11 vert. per in. (93.5 per sq. in.).
Color: 7, red, medium blue, light blue, medium green, tan, dark brown, ivory.
Condition: rewoven areas in field and borders, upper border rewoven, no original ends or selvedges.
Unpublished.

52

XII
Anatolia, 17th-early 18th century
The Textile Museum, R 34.22.1

Triple arches with a higher central unit were widely used in Roman architecture and the form was adopted by the Muslims who used it occasionally in their palaces and in their mosques. The oldest known representation of this device on prayer rugs is seen on two 16th century Ottoman court-designed rugs, the Metropolitan rug (no. I) and a large fragment in Bucharest (all-wool; Beattie 1968, fig. 3 & fn. 7). Both have the higher central arch supported by paired columns and above a crenelated frieze with blossoms. Court rugs of this type must have inspired the Anatolian weavers to adapt the curvilinear drawing of the model to their own preference for angular outlines and bold colors. One element of the design which lacks a surviving court prototype is the use of large lanceolate leaves in the spandrels. That such leaves were known in 17th century Istanbul is confirmed by an inventory of the Valide Mosque which describes three Persian rugs with designs of "saz," long curved, serrated leaves (Beattie 1968, p. 246). The floral cartouches of the main border are characteristic of this specific rug type, the dating of which has been greatly assisted by its representation in Netherlandish paintings during the 17th century. The rug in Nicolaes van Gelder's *Still Life*, painted in 1664, shows the same capitals, columns, lanceolate leaf decorated spandrels, crenelated frieze, and main border (p. 131, Fig. 21).

While May Beattie believes a 17th century date is possible for some of these rugs, she disassociates their production from the Ladiks on technical grounds (discussed under no. XVI). She concludes that their provenance can only be considered in conjunction with the many closely related prayer rugs preserved in Transylvanian churches and with rugs which she believes come from widely separate areas in Anatolia (Beattie 1968, pp. 251-255). Ellis agrees that they are not from Ladik but also is uncertain whether rugs of this particular type were made in Anatolia or in European Turkey (unpublished).

Size: L. 1.68m (5' 6'') × W. 1.117m (3' 8 '').
Warp: wool, pale red, 2 Z-yarns S-plied.
Weft: wool, pale red, Z-yarns, 2 shots.
Pile: wool, 2 Z-yarns, Gördes knot, 9 horiz. × 10 vert. per in. (90 per sq. in.).
Color: 8, red, dark blue, medium blue, light blue, yellow, ivory, blue-green, brown-black.
Condition: woven top end first, some worn areas repaired, brown-black partially disintegrated and replaced, lower border cut and replaced by side border from another rug, no original ends or selvedges.
Published: Mackie, no. 41, illus.; Yohe & Jones, no. 13, illus.; Jacoby, Taf. 46.

XIII
Turkey, late 17th-early 18th century
Loaned by The Dumbarton Oaks Collection, 14

While no. XII and this rug both developed from Ottoman court-designed rugs, specific aspects of this rug suggest a different prototype and also a different provenance. The columns' bases were derived from the type seen on the Metropolitan rug (no. I); however, an earlier model for the double crowns of the side niches is not known. The spacious proportions of the spandrels in which large lanceolate leaves frame a cog-wheel rosette, a device which also occurs on no. XII, appear to have limited the space allotted to the crenelated frieze with flowers. A display of the favorite Turkish flowers, tulips, carnations and forget-me-nots, forms an uncommon main border pattern.

In contrast to the bold, vivid coloring of no. XII, this particular rug has muted tones. It is also distinguished by its thick construction and weight and therefore bears no physical resemblance to the examples of the stylistic class which no. XII clearly exemplifies. These unusual features have caused Ellis to suggest (in conversation) that this rug was not made in Anatolia, but in Transylvania, if not in nearby European Turkey. Today, the greatest concentration of similar rugs appears to be in Budapest.

Size: L. 1.53m (5' 1/4'') × W. 1.27m (4' 2'').
Warp: wool, ivory 2 Z-yarns S-plied, 2 warp levels, ends dyed yellow.
Weft: wool, red, Z-yarns, 2 shots, lazy lines.
Pile: wool, 1 Z-yarn, Gördes knot (slant to left), 8 horiz. × 10 vert. per in. (80 per sq. in.).
Color: 8, deep red, medium red, medium blue, mustard, yellow, beige, brown-black, ivory.
Condition: woven top end first, scattered rewoven areas, black-brown mostly disintegrated and replaced by tan or by grey for 2 large lanceolate leaves in spandrels, ends: weft-faced plain weave, yellow wool (ravelled off); selvedges: red wool, 4 cord (single warps), attached by ground weft around second inside warp.
Published: Mackie, no. 42, illus.; Yohe & Jones, no. 14, illus.

56

Detail of one side of the niche from the back. The red wefts of the rug are only discontinuous in the niche area where they are replaced by ivory wefts. The meeting points of the discontinuous wefts occur in the guard stripes adjacent to the niche and form an irregular saw-tooth on each side. Photograph courtesy the St. Louis Art Museum.

XIV
Gördes, late 18th-early 19th century
Loaned by The St. Louis Art Museum, Gift of James F. Ballard, 79:1929

One of the largest groups of Turkish prayer rugs comprises those traditionally attributed to the looms of Gördes (Ghiordes). These, however, show sufficient stylistic and technical differences as to defy the possibility of one shared provenance. The example illustrated here representing the purest type of Gördes prayer rug displays a niche whose arch is formed by finely stepped diagonals; a horizontal panel above the spandrels and one below the niche; and multiple borders with the main one displaying a compressed version of that on the late 16th century Ottoman court manufactory rugs (no. I). Two decorated vertical bands often appear instead of columns. Flowers are displayed across the bottom of the niche as on the Ottoman court rugs (nos. I, V). The introduction of a floral motif in the arch probably replaces the earlier representation of a hanging mosque lamp (nos. I, III, VI and p. 129, Fig. 18). The spandrel decoration of a blossoming branch is also dependent upon earlier court models (p. 130, Fig. 20).

In addition to the stylistic dependence on the Ottoman court manufactory rugs, two technical features appear to have continued, the surprisingly tight weave with over 200 knots per square inch, and the use of ivory cotton for details in the design. Only the selvedges are silk. A subtle and identifying new feature is the replacement of the red weft by an ivory weft in the niche; this occurs in the guard stripes adjacent to the niche and

while it is extremely obvious from the back (see detail of XIV), it is sometimes visible also from the front of the rug.

Later Gördes rugs are characterized by novel coloring and an increased use of ivory cotton for the design and for the weft. When there is a color change in the weft, it is often highly irregular and illogical. Many of the rugs with these features are attributed to early 20th century manufacture in Bandirma (Panderma) and other copying centers.

Size: L. 1.855m (6′ 1′′) × W. 1.372m (4′ 6′′).
Warp: wool, ivory, 2 Z-yarns S-plied, alternate warps slightly depressed, ends dyed light blue.
Weft: wool, red, Z-yarns, 2 shots; cotton, ivory, 2 Z-yarns, 2 shots (behind niche only), lazy lines.
Pile: wool, 1 Z-yarn (polychrome and ivory); cotton, 1 Z-yarn (ivory, small details only); Gördes knot (slant to left), 12 horiz. × 19 vert. per in. (228 per sq. in.).
Color: 11, maroon, red, rose, deep blue, medium blue, blue-green, pale yellow, tan, deep brown, black, ivory.
Condition: woven top end first, occasional re-knotted areas, deep brown and black disintegrating, heading: light blue wool, weft-faced plain weave; finish: red wool, weft-faced plain weave; no original selvedges.
Published: Dimand 1935, pl. XXXVI; MacLean & Blair, no. 24.

XIV

XV
Anatolia, 18th century

Loaned by The St. Louis Art Museum, Gift of James F. Ballard, 82:1929

Although this type of rug has been frequently attributed to Gördes, it is so unlike the true Gördes type, as exemplified by no. XIV, both in its design and construction that it warrants separate consideration. A horseshoe-shaped arch, which is sometimes supported by columns, dominates the usually undecorated red field. The spandrel is apt to display a stylized rendition of a scrolling vine whose model is undoubtedly that represented by the Ottoman court manufactory prayer rug fragment in Istanbul (Ellis 1969, fig. 2). A single horizontal panel located above the spandrels is characteristic of these rugs. The spacing of the border designs is more in keeping with the 16th century style than the compressed drawing seen on the true Gördes rugs. In addition to the above stylistic differences, these rugs have fewer than 100 knots per square inch and there is no color change in the weft beside the niche.

Many of these horseshoe-arch rugs have been preserved in Protestant churches in the Transylvanian Alps in Rumania, formerly part of Hungary. Some bear an 18th century date; the year 1736 was embroidered on one rug possibly when it was given to a church (Schmutzler, Taf. 33, color; Erdmann 1970, fig. 216). The exact place of manufacture remains uncertain. At least one scholar believes they were made in Transylvania or nearby in 17th century European Turkey (Ellis 1969, p. 19).

Size: L. 1.78m (5' 10'') × W. 1.22m (4').
Warp: wool, ivory, 2 Z-yarns S-plied, alternate warps depressed, ends dyed red.
Weft: wool, very pale red, Z-yarns, 2 shots; wool, light browns, loose Z-yarns, 2 shots, lazy lines.
Pile: wool, 1 Z-yarn, Gördes knot, 8.5 horiz. × 10 vert. per in. (85 per sq. in.).
Color: 8, red, light red, medium blue, deep blue, brown, ivory, 2 fugitive dyes now tan and pale yellow.
Condition: woven top end first, reknotted areas in center of niche and all of upper left including part of spandrel, horiz. panel, top and side border, bottom guard also partially reknotted, no original ends or selvedges.
Published: Dimand 1935, pl. XXXIX; MacLean & Blair, no. 29.

XV

XVI
Ladik, Konya province, 19th century
Loaned by The St. Louis Art Museum, Gift of
James F. Ballard, 94:1929

Among the few Ladiks bearing late 18th century dates, two types of columnless niches appear, one a stepped single niche, the other a tripartite niche. Although floral motifs are sometimes introduced into the field of the niche, the typical features of these rugs include an undecorated field, large serrated leaves and stylized blossoms in the spandrels, and a horizontal frieze bearing crenelations and long stemmed tulips. Prototypes for a horizontal panel appear on the Mamluk prayer rug (p. 130, Fig. 19) and the Ottoman court rug (no. 1). The frieze is placed either above the spandrels or beneath the niche, in which case the tulips are upside down. Both the coloring and drawing are usually very bold. The most common main border pattern is composed of rosettes alternating with stylized tulips (Denny, p. 10, figs. 4-6), with an isolated horizontal bar sometimes inserted between the flowers. The larger flanking stripes display an angular vine motif. The presence of numerous stripes is characteristic of several types of 18th-19th century Turkish rugs. In spite of the dated examples, the dating of many Ladik rugs is problematical partially due to their sturdy nature and excellent condition. They have been traditionally ascribed to the same weaving center as the triple-arch rugs (no.

XII); however, Beattie has pointed out certain technical variations which indicate different weaving centers. Lazy lines occur in triple-arch rugs but not in Ladiks; purple is not found in triple-arch rugs but is frequent in Ladiks. Beattie continues to attribute such "Ladiks" as this rug to Ladik, near Konya, where, as she points out, village women still weave this pattern (Beattie 1968, pp. 253, 254).

Size: L. 1.88m (6' 2'') × W. 1.168m (3' 10'').
Warp: wool, ivory, 2 Z-yarns S-plied, alternate warps depressed.
Weft: wool, ivory, Z-yarns, 2 shots, no lazy lines.
Pile: wool, 2 Z-yarns, Gördes knot (slant to left), 7.5 horiz. × 11.5 vert. per in. (86 per sq. in.).
Color: 10, red, barn red, yellow-tan, tan, brown, brown-black, light green, medium blue, deep blue, ivory.
Condition: woven top end first, very good except brown-black in end guards partially missing, no original ends, selvedges: red and pale salmon wool, 2 cord, attached by ground weft around inside cord.
Published: Dimand 1935, pl. XLVII; MacLean & Blair, no. 54.

XVI

XVII
Kula, 19th century
Loaned by The St. Louis Art Museum, Gift of
James F. Ballard, 85:1929

Of the several styles of prayer rugs attributed
to Kula, one popular type appears to have developed from the earlier triple-arch prayer rugs
(nos. I, XII). While columns are present on some of
these rugs (Dimand 1935, pl. XLII), the use of two
decorated vertical bands connected with the spandrels is more common. Linear or floral motifs tend
to encroach on the space allotted to the side arches,
especially in later examples. In contrast to the
strong colors of this rug, most Kulas display a
medium blue ground and several tones of muted
yellow and tan. The latter are the result of fugitive
dyes which often render the original pattern illegi-
ble. The repetition of a single flower usually patterns the spandrels, above which a horizontal panel
is seen. Occasionally Kulas also have a second
panel located beneath the niche. Several narrow
guard stripes flank the main border which often
displays symmetrically drawn, stylized blossoming
plants. They are frequently upside down in relation
to the niche. Other border designs include one

based on that of the 16th century rug (no. I) and one
with approximately twelve narrow guard stripes of
equal width (Erdmann 1962, fig. 164).

Size: L. 1.905m (6' 3'') × W. 1.295m (4' 3'').
Warp: wool, pale yellow, 2 Z-yarns S-plied, alternate warps very depressed.
Weft: wool, ivory, medium brown, dark brown
(each used separately), I-yarns, 2 shots, lazy lines.
Pile: wool, 1 I-yarn, Gördes knot (slant to left), 8
horiz. × 11 vert. per in. (88 per sq. in.).
Color: 8, deep red, medium blue, deep blue, dark
brown, black, ivory, 2 shades tan probably fugitive
dyes.
Condition: woven top end first, fugitive dyes typical this rug group, bottom outer guard missing, no
original ends, selvedges: tan wool, 2 cord, attached
by ground weft around inside cord.
Published: Dimand 1935, pl. XLI; MacLean &
Blair, no. 35.

64

XVII

XVIII
Mujur, early 19th century
Loaned by The St. Louis Art Museum, Gift of
James F. Ballard, 108:1929

Although Mujur prayer rugs are characterized by rather coarse weaving with fewer than
70 knots per square inch, this classic example
boasts strong, angular drawing complemented by
rich, vibrant colors. A stepped arch identifies the
niche whose interior outline is usually edged with
carnations and, on this rug, with polychromatic
zigzags as well. While very large stylized leaves
sometimes fill the spandrels (Dimand 1973, fig.
208), two large ewers, associated with the ablutions performed before prayer, may appear instead. The crenelated frieze above the spandrels is
another example of the honored continuity of earlier designs (nos. I, XII, XVI, and p. 129, Fig. 18).
Isolated units form the pattern of the main border;
a diamond with corner brackets encloses two con-
centric stars. The fanciful variation of colors disguises the otherwise repetitive nature of this unit.
The design of connected diamonds on the wider
inner guard stripe is typical of these rugs whereas
that of the wider outer guard stripe is less common.

While most 16th and 17th century Turkish
prayer rugs were woven from the bottom of the
design, many 18th and most 19th century rugs
were started at the top. In this rug, the design unit
forming the main border illustrates this situation;
insufficient space remained in the side borders for
the completion of the motif when it became neces-
sary to begin the main border across the bottom.
An additional spacing problem occurred in the
main border at both ends resulting in the introduction of three small octagons.

Size: L. 1.778m (5'10'') × W. 1.345m (4'5'').
Warp: wool, ivory, 2 Z-yarns S-plied.
Weft: wool, red, Z-yarns, 2 shots.
Pile: wool, 2 Z-yarns, occasionally 3 Z-yarns
(ivory), Gördes knot (slant to right and slant to
left), 7.5 horiz. × 8.5 vert. per in. (64 per sq. in.).
Color: 11, rich red, red, lavender, medium blue,
blue-green, light green, mustard, light brown,
tan, brown-black, ivory.
Condition: woven top end first, worn areas,
brown-black disintegrating, upper left corner
outer guard reknotted, bottom outer guard missing, no original ends, selvedges: green wool, 3
cord, attached by ground weft around inside cord.
Published: Dimand 1935, pl. LVII; MacLean &
Blair, no. 80.

XVIII

XIX
Konya Area, early 19th century
Loaned by Mrs. Harper Sibley

Several 19th century triple-arch prayer rugs are known but rarely are the proportions, clarity of design, and color balance as successful as on this rug. The stylistic dependence of these rugs on the earlier triple-arch rugs is clearly evident. Similarities between this rug and nos. I and XII appear in the column bases, capitals, triangular unit above the impost block, two huge leaves encircling a linear motif in the spandrels, details of the crenelated frieze with stylized tulips, as well as the use of color. Even the inner guard stripe displays the small isolated blossoms which occur on earlier rugs. The large connected rosettes of the main border also appear on a single-arch rug which is related to this group and which is dated 1237 (1822 A.D.) (Schürmann 1966, p. 20r., color).

Size: L. 1.78m (5'10¼'') × W. 1.08m (3'6½'').
Warp: wool, ivory, 2 Z-yarns S-plied.
Weft: wool, pale red, Z-yarns, 2 shots (sometimes 3 or 4), no lazy lines.
Pile: wool, 2 Z-yarns, Gördes knot, 7 horiz. × 8 vert. per in. (56 per sq. in.).
Color: 8, red, maroon, dark green, royal blue, yellow, tan, brown-black, ivory.
Condition: woven bottom end first, numerous worn areas, many reknotted areas, ends: remnant of red wool, weft-faced plain weave (fringe is modern); no original selvedges.
Unpublished.

XIX

XX
Milas, 19th century

Loaned by the Philadelphia Museum of Art, The Samuel S. White, 3rd, and Vera White Collection, 67-30-310

The shape of the arch of the niche is the identifying feature of this group of prayer rugs and is believed to be a stylized rendition of the horseshoe-arch seen in no. XV and Fig. 20 (p. 130). Other design elements which may appear on these rugs include: a triangular indentation at the bottom of the niche with "fringed" diamonds above; the edging of the interior outline of the niche with small blossoms; and stylized blossoms superimposed on vines bearing trilobed leaves in the spandrels. The prototype of the latter combination occurs frequently in 16th century Ottoman court art (Denny, p. 11, figs. 8, 9). The same blossom and trilobed leaf also appear in the main border pattern which was derived from an earlier version seen on the 18th century horseshoe-arch rug, no. XV. While this is only one of several main border patterns found on these rugs, the designs used on the inner and outer guard stripes are considerably less varied.

Size: L. 1.677m (5'6'') × W. 1.156m (3'9½'').
Warp: wool, ivory, some ivory and brown, 2 Z-yarns S-plied.
Weft: wool, red, Z-yarns, 2 shots.
Pile: wool, 2 Z-yarns, Gördes knot (slant to left), 8 horiz. × 10.5 vert. per in. (84 per sq. in.).
Color: 8, brick red, coral red, purple, medium blue, light green, yellow-tan, dark brown, ivory.
Condition: woven bottom end first, dark brown disintegrating, small area of upper left corner reknotted, ends: red wool, weft-faced plain weave; selvedges: red wool, 4 cords of 2 warps.
Unpublished.

70

XX

XXI
Anatolia, 18th-early 19th century
Loaned by the St. Louis Art Museum, Gift of
James F. Ballard, 109:1930

While most Turkish prayer rugs in Western collections can be grouped into known types, this rug stands apart. The bold outline of the red niche with its two abrupt indentations on each side is very unusual. A single indentation on each side characterizes Milas rugs (no. XX). Only occasionally do rugs appear with several large indentations on each side (Schürmann 1966, p. 20 r.; Erdmann 1962, fig. 162). A small repeated motif, possibly here a stylized tulip, edges the interior outline of the niche which softens the severity of its profile. This is a characteristic feature of several types of 18th-19th century Anatolian rugs (e.g., Milas). The six horizontal motifs displayed on the ivory ground of the spandrels are very original and defy certain identification; they may have developed from large serrated leaves (cf. McMullan, pl. 107; Yohe & Jones, fig. 62). The boldness of their drawing and coloring complements that of the niche. In comparison, the main border design of floral cartouches on a yellow ground appears noticeably

weak. Both this border design and that of the inner guard stripe are known from other Anatolian rugs, such as the 17th century triple-arch rug (no. XII).

Analysis courtesy of Charles Grant Ellis.
Size: L. 1.422m (4'8'') × W. 0.965m (3'2'').
Warp: wool, ivory (with occasional dark fibers), 2 Z-yarns S-plied, alternate warps slightly depressed.
Weft: wool, ivory (with occasional dark fibers, some blue), Z-yarns, 2 shots.
Pile: wool, Z-yarn, Gördes knot (slant to left), 10.5 horiz. × 12 vert. per in. (126 per sq. in.).
Color: 9, red, light red, violet, dull pink, medium blue, blue-green, yellow, black-brown, ivory.
Condition: woven bottom end first, extensive re-knotting especially in field of rug, outer guard stripe missing on all 4 sides, no original ends or selvedges.
Published: Dimand 1935, pl. LVI.

72

XXI

XXII
Anatolia, 19th century
Anonymous Loan

Discovering unfamiliar combinations of familiar design motifs is one of the pleasures of studying Islamic rugs, especially when their layout and color scheme are well balanced. The red field of the stepped-arch niche displays a diamond-shaped medallion and small scattered octagons. The two large, stylized foliate motifs beneath probably developed from comparable representations on an earlier type of Anatolian prayer rug (i.e., nos. VIII, IX) (e.g., Zick, Abb. 6g). Their location on this rug, however, has generated the belief that they indicate the position for the feet of the faithful during prayer. Such representations do appear on prayer rugs, especially from Turkey (e.g., p. 20, Fig. 9; Erdmann 1962, figs. 152, 155). The presence of corner brackets at the bottom of the niche is infrequent on prayer rugs although an earlier example occurs on a multiple-niche prayer rug (no. VII). While octagons are certainly familiar motifs on Anatolian rugs, dating from the earliest known Islamic rugs of the 13th century which were found in Konya (Erdmann 1970, pp. 41 ff.), the triangular extension on each large octagon in the blue spandrels is

unusual. Occasionally rugs appear which display two distinct and unrelated designs patterning different portions of one area, as seen here in the pale yellow ground of the main border. The isolated rosettes of the inner guard stripe are noteworthy as they clearly illustrate the traditional continuity of patterns; they also formed the inner guard stripes of the Ottoman court-designed prayer rugs (nos. I, III, IV).

Size: L. 1.69m (5'6½'') × W. 1.215m (4').
Warp: wool, ivory, 2 Z-yarns S-plied.
Weft: wool, red, Z-yarns, 2 or 3 shots, sometimes 5 shots.
Pile: wool, 2 Z-yarns, Gördes knot, 7 horiz. × 7 vert. per in. (49 per sq. in.).
Color: 7, red, magenta, medium blue, medium green, pale yellow, brown-black, ivory.
Condition: woven bottom end first, pile worn at bottom of field, brown-black disintegrating, ends: red wool, weft-faced plain weave, 2 rows of 2-strand weft twining; selvedges not original.
Unpublished.

XXII

PRAYER RUGS
OF MUGHAL INDIA

The Mughal dynasty was founded by Babur (1526-1530), a fifth genera-
tion descendant of the Mongol ruler Timur or Tamerlane. Babur brought
Persian culture and art to India. The court rugs of this period were doubtless
imported from Persia. Babur's son and successor, Humayun (1530-1556),
who spent some time at the court of Shah Tahmasp in Tabriz, invited two
famous Persian painters, Mir Sayyid Ali and Abdus Samad, to join his court
in India. He commissioned them to illustrate the Persian Romance of Amir
Hamza, the story of the uncle of the Prophet. The illustrations of large size
were painted by a number of Mughal artists on cotton cloth. The illustrations of the twelve large volumes of Amir Hamza were not completed until
the reign of Humayun's son and successor, Akbar the Great (1556-1605).

Many of the paintings of Amir Hamza depict contemporary rugs which
to a great extent were of Persian origin or Mughal copies recalling the
Safavid medallion and floral rugs. Abul Fazl, the historian of Akbar, tells us
that the emperor "caused carpets to be made of wonderful varieties and
charming textures; he has appointed experienced workmen, who have
produced many masterpieces. The carpets of Iran and Turan (Turkestan)
are no more thought of, although merchants still import carpets from
Jushagan, Kerman, Khuzistan (in western Persia), and Sabzawar (in
Khurasan). All kinds of carpet weavers have settled here, and drive a
flourishing trade. These are to be found in every town, but especially in
Agra, Fatehpur Sikri and Lahore."

Akbar's son, Jahangir (1605-1628), was an eminent patron of the arts.
Artists working for Jahangir painted beautiful specimens of Indian birds,
animals and flowers, particularly in Kashmir, which was called "the garden
of eternal spring." Mansur, one of the court artists of Jahangir, produced
more than one hundred paintings of Kashmir flowers. Some of the rugs
made under Jahangir, chiefly at Lahore, were no doubt designed by his
court painters, such as Mansur, Manohar and Murad. Jahangir's Mughal
style is apparent in a number of large and small rugs. Two large rugs,
formerly in the Lord Sackville collection, are now in the Metropolitan
Museum of Art. Pictorial rugs with naturalistic floral and animal decoration
are in the Boston Museum of Fine Arts, the famous Peacock rug in the
Austrian Museum of Applied Arts, in Vienna, and an animal rug with
hunting scenes in the Widener collection of the National Gallery of Art,
Washington.

Prayer rugs with floral decoration were made in the time of Jahangir. The court weavers produced not only knotted prayer rugs of wool, but also of silk brocades, velvets, and embroidered cottons (Victoria and Albert Museum). Some of the court painters of Jahangir made cartoons for prayer rugs, showing a niche with a single large plant. Such cartoons are included in several albums assembled in the time of Jahangir and his successor, Shah Jahan. To the period of Jahangir may be attributed a splendid woolen prayer rug formerly in the Aynard collection in Lyon, and now in the collection of Baron Thyssen Bornemisza in Switzerland. The niche of the rug contains a large naturalistic tree with leaves and large lily-like blossoms. At each side of the central plant are smaller plants with blossoms.

The Mughal style of weaving rugs and textiles was fully developed in the time of Shah Jahan (1628-1658), the son and successor of Jahangir. The naturalistic style of decoration in rugs and textiles reached its height in the court workshops of Shah Jahan. In some of the rugs, the design was still inspired by Persian rugs of the Herat type, but modified by the introduction of naturalistic plants and flowers peculiar to India. Other rugs show a floral design entirely Mughal in style, consisting of rows of flowering plants, including roses, iris, carnations, lilies and peonies, rendered in naturalistic style. A splendid early example, formerly in the Kevorkian collection, is now in the Metropolitan Museum of Art. Other examples are in the Jaipur Museum, the J. Paul Getty collection and the Victoria and Albert Museum.

Prayer rugs of wool and silk were also made in the time of Shah Jahan. A fine prayer rug of that period in the collection of Joseph V. McMullan has a large plant filling the whole niche and bearing naturalistic leaves and large chrysanthemum-like blossoms. The plant grows from a hill and is accompanied by small tulip-like plants. The typical Mughal arch has floral scrolls in the spandrels which are also repeated in the border. A similar floral design appears in a contemporary fine velvet, formerly in the collection of Paravicini of Cairo. Silk prayer rugs were also made in the time of Shah Jahan but only very few survived. A fragment of such a rug is in the Altman Collection of the Metropolitan Museum. It originally had a niche resting on columns and showing a hilly ground with small flowering plants and a large central plant with thistle-like leaves. It is extremely fine in technique having approximately 2552 knots to the square inch.

The manufacture of fine rugs continued in the time of Shah Jahan's successor, Aurangzib (1658-1707). To the end of the seventeenth century can be assigned a splendid *mille-fleurs* prayer rug in the Austrian Museum of Applied Arts, Vienna. Its niche resting on cypress trees is filled with a splendid bouquet of assorted flowers rendered in rich colors.   M.S.D.

XXIII
Mughal, first half 17th century
Loaned by The Metropolitan Museum of Art, Bequest of Joseph V. McMullan, 1974, 1974.149.2

The solemnity and grandeur of one large, naturalistically drawn plant, possibly here a chrysanthemum, are characteristic of 17th century Mughal court art. Similar representations exist not only in manuscripts and in textiles but also in the marble facades of palaces and mausolea where semi-precious stones often form the plant. On this rug, the symmetrically drawn plant grows on a blossom-sprinkled hillock from which two tulips also grow. Several features of this rug are identifying Mughal characteristics: the foliate outline of the cusped arch; the self-contained nature of the chrysanthemum scroll in the spandrels; and an indication of the center of each side of the main border pattern by a specific design variation, in this case a blossom drawn in profile. The specific color tones used in this rug and the tone-on-tone silhouettes executed here in the characteristic pink on red and tan on ivory are hallmarks of 17th century Mughal rug weaving.

The importance of this rug becomes further apparent upon recalling that this is one of only three surviving single-plant 17th century Mughal knotted prayer rugs. The finest of the three is undoubtedly the Pincket rug (p. 132, Fig. 22) whose exquisitely delicate design, which has been achieved by the use of approximately 2000 woolen Senneh knots per square inch, represents the best

royal art of the period. The Aynard prayer rug, which is probably a *saff* fragment, in the Thyssen-Bornemisza collection (p. 132, Fig. 23) also displays superior drawing and weaving (Beattie 1972, p. 67 & pl. IX, color).

As a result of several surprisingly similar compositional and stylistic features on certain Ottoman and Mughal court prayer rugs, Ellis has suggested that Ottoman court prayer rugs may have been available in the Mughal court as models (Ellis 1969, p. 18).

Size: L. 1.55m (5'1'') × W. 1.03m (3'4½'').
Warp: cotton, ivory, 4 and 7 Z-yarns S-plied, alternate warps very depressed.
Weft: shots nos. 1 and 3, cotton, ivory, 2 Z-yarns; shot no. 2, silk, red, I-yarn.
Pile: wool, 3 or 4 Z-yarns, Senneh knot open on the left, 15 horiz. × 15 vert. per in. (225 per sq. in.).
Color: 10, crimson, rose, blue-green, dark blue, tan, light tan, brown, light brown, aubergine, ivory.
Condition: woven bottom end first, reknotting along central axis of rug and few other areas, no original ends or selvedges.
Published: Dimand 1973, fig. 139; Ettinghausen 1970, pl. 15, color; Ellis 1969, p. 18; McMullan, pl. 7, color; Welch, pl. 56; Dilley, pl. XXXII.

XXIII

Full view of Indian *saff*.

XXIV
Multiple-Niche Prayer Rug or Saff, Mughal India, 18th century
The Textile Museum, R 63.00.15

Multiple-niche prayer rugs from Mughal India are rarely preserved. A six-niche fragment is in the collection of the Islamic Museum, West Berlin (Erdmann 1970, pl. XIV, color, incorrectly called "Persian"; Ellis 1969, p. 18, called "Mughal India"). A two-niche fragment in the Metropolitan Museum of Art is considered by many scholars to be a Mughal fragment from a larger *saff* (no. XXVI). A single-niche rug in the Thyssen-Bornemisza collection (p. 132, Fig. 23) is believed to have originally been part of a multiple-niche prayer rug (Beattie 1972, p. 67, pl. IX, color). Although the illustrated *saff* is believed to have been woven at a later date than the above mentioned rugs, it exhibits certain stylistic features reminiscent of the refined sophistication of 17th century Mughal court art. A simplified, pointed arch terminating in a palmette is supported by columns whose bases and capitals are clearly defined. The arches, the grounds of the niches and the spandrels are rendered in different colors: Indian crimson, medium blue, dark blue, dark blue-green, and mustard. Several different types of designs pattern the fields of the niches as are also seen on the West Berlin and Metropolitan *saff* fragments. Those on this rug include isolated flowering plants, a continuous lattice framing a five-petalled, ivory flower, and an all over, non-directional, floral and foliate design which ap-

pears as though it may have been adopted from a larger surface. The treatment of the spandrels on this rug, on the other hand, is nearly uniform. A vine bears a variety of leaves and blossoms. The main stripe which separates the seven niches also serves as a guard stripe. It displays a continuous vine bearing crimson roses on an ivory ground. Part of the main border pattern, a crimson and tan reciprocal trefoil, is visible above the niches.

Size: L. 6.158m (20'2'') (warp) × W. 1.38m (4'6½'') (weft).
Warp: cotton, ivory, 4 Z-yarns S-plied, alternate warps depressed.
Weft: cotton, tan, 2 Z-yarns, 3 shots.
Pile: wool, 2 Z-yarns, Senneh knot open on the left (slant to left), 9 horiz. × 9 vert. per in. (81 per sq. in.).
Color: 11, crimson, rose, dark blue, medium blue, dark blue-green, green, mustard, brown, tan, buff, ivory.
Condition: woven left end first, no evidence to indicate original size of rug; ends reknotted, lower main border missing, upper border without selvedge; numerous repaired tears and reknotted areas.
Published: *Textile Museum Journal*, Vol. II, No. 4 (1969), p. 55, illus.

80

XXV
Multiple-Niche Prayer Rug or Saff,
Mughal India, early 18th century
Loaned by Edmund de Unger

The Mughal predilection for portraying one large, naturalistically rendered flowering plant within a niche was not limited to 17th century use only but also continued during the 18th century. Of the two types of flowering plants seen on this multiple-niche prayer rug, the central plant is particularly reminiscent of those portrayed by 17th century Mughal court artists (no. XXIII and p. 132, Figs. 22 & 23, latter is believed to be a *saff* fragment). The majestic scale and drawing of the earlier representations have been lost however. The semi-stylized plants on this *saff* no longer grow from a flower-sprinkled hillock, although the pair of tulips which flank the 17th century plants continue to be present. A particularly striking feature of this rug is the representation of the niches; they appear as a continuous arcade. The lobed and pointed arches spring from a shared impost block, column, and base. The continuity is partially interrupted by the vertical extensions above the impost block and the "fringed," small, lobed medallions. Gracefully rendered blossoms pattern the spandrels. The main border displays continuous vines bearing a variety of leaves and blossoms.

The motif in the flanking guard stripes, an angular S, also appears in the 18th century *saff*, no. XXIV. Although the proportions of these niches may appear vertically compressed in comparison with those on many prayer rugs, they seem to share the same proportions as those on two other Mughal *saffs*, no. XXVI and the West Berlin six-niche fragment (Ellis 1969, fig. 25).

Two other rugs with seemingly identical designs are known, a seven-niche rug (Ellis 1969, fig. 27) and another three-niche piece in the de Unger collection.

Analysis courtesy of Friedrich Spuhler.
Size: L. 2.60m (8'6½'') (warp) × W. 1.31m (4'3½'') (weft).
Warp: cotton, white, 4 S-yarns Z-plied.
Weft: cotton, white, 2 and 3 Z-yarns.
Pile: wool, 3 Z-yarns, Senneh knot open on the left, 11 × 8.75 per in. (96.25 per sq. in.).
Color: 6, cherry-red, bright yellow, pale green, dark blue, dark brown, white.
Condition: considerable reknotting.
Unpublished.

82

PRAYER RUGS OF PERSIA (IRAN)

The earliest known representation of a Persian prayer rug appears in a Timurid miniature of 1436 in the Bibliothèque Nationale, Paris. The arch of the niche is lobed and the field has an all over pattern of squares containing rosettes. In the spandrels are floral motifs, while the narrow border has a wavy scroll. The prayer rug recalls fifteenth century prayer niches of faience mosaics, several of which are in various museums, including the Metropolitan Museum of Art.

The prayer rugs of the Safavid period follow the decoration of sixteenth and seventeenth century rugs in general. To the Shah Tahmasp period (1524-1576) can be assigned a prayer rug in the Metropolitan Museum of Art, showing a mihrab filled with typical Safavid floral scrolls and Chinese cloud bands. The spandrels of the arch are divided into irregular panels filled with Koranic inscriptions. The border of this prayer rug shows a characteristic Safavid design of arabesques interlaced with floral scrolls. In addition, there are, in the upper part of the border, Koranic inscriptions. The color scheme and technique of this rug, recalling many rugs of the Tabriz looms, could not be much later than the middle of the sixteenth century. There is a whole group of prayer rugs which are often wrongly classified as sixteenth century Safavid, which are, however, eighteenth and even nineteenth century copies made in Turkish court looms. They differ considerably in color and details of the ornament from the sixteenth century prayer rugs in the Metropolitan Museum of Art and other collections. A later sixteenth century prayer rug, also in the Metropolitan Museum of Art, has a mihrab filled with semi-naturalistic trees and shrubs. In the apex of the niche, is, instead of a mosque lamp, a vase with flowers. The Koranic inscriptions are confined to the border only. The more vivid colors and the style in general indicate that this rug was made in another rug center, possibly Kashan, famous for its silk brocades and silk rugs.

In the time of Shah Abbas the Great (1587-1629), some luxurious prayer rugs were made in the court looms of Isfahan. Two multiple-niche rugs are preserved at the shrine of Imam Ali at Nejev, near Kufa, in Iraq. Both are of wool with brocading in gold and silver. One has three mihrabs; the other, incomplete, has six and part of a seventh. Both prayer rugs are richly decorated with floral scrolls, interlaced arabesques and cloud bands, rendered in rich and brilliant colors. The style of these rugs recalls the Shah Abbas silk rugs, also brocaded with gold and silver thread, which are attributed either to the looms of Isfahan or Kashan. Of historical importance is the inscription of the first prayer rug: "Donated by the dog of this shrine Abbas," no doubt Shah Abbas I or the Great. A border of a woolen rug in the same shrine also bears an identical inscription. There is little doubt that these prayer rugs, made especially for the shrine of Imam Ali, were the products of Isfahan looms, where some of the finest silk rugs of the Shah Abbas period were made.

A later Persian prayer rug, probably of the second half of the seventeenth century, is in the Metropolitan Museum of Art. It is a prayer rug with two mihrabs, one above the other. They are decorated with rows of tulip-like plants and floral scrolls with lanceolate leaves which resemble rugs attributed to Herat in the province of Khurasan.

Eighteenth century prayer rugs with floral decoration, the so-called *mille-fleurs* rugs, were made in the district of Shiraz, in the province of Fars. They show a dense floral pattern with numerous stylized or semi-naturalistic blossoms growing out of a vase and filling out the whole field. The arches of the niches rest on cypress trees with pedestals. The color of the niche is usually red, the spandrels are in contrasting colors, such as yellow or red. The floral design of the spandrels either repeats the pattern of the field or is drawn on a larger scale. One of the prayer rugs in the McMullan collection has a more naturalistic floral pattern of the yellow field, consisting of roses, irises, carnations and other blossoms growing out of a vase. The spandrels of this prayer rug are red with a floral pattern similar to that of the field. These prayer rugs are sometimes wrongly attributed to India. Their similarities with floral rugs made in the district of Shiraz in the time of Shah Kerim Khan (1750-1779) of the Zand dynasty, leave little doubt that these prayer rugs were of Persian manufacture. They show also a similarity with rugs made by the Kashgai tribe of the Shiraz district.

During the nineteenth century, prayer rugs were made in various districts of Persia, such as Kashan, the province of Khurassan and Kurdistan. The town of Senne in the province of Ardalan produced fine rugs with a small floral all over pattern. Famous were the Senne kilims with delicate floral design, related to those of the knotted variety. Among the Senne kilims are also prayer rugs, which are represented in various collections, including that of Joseph V. McMullan.   M.S.D.

XXVI
Multiple-Niche Prayer Rug or Saff, Persia or Mughal India, 17th century

Loaned by The Metropolitan Museum of Art, Gift of James F. Ballard, 22.100.72

In contrast to the extremely fine and prolific production of large rugs designed and woven under the auspices of the 16th and 17th century Safavid rulers, it appears, based on survival rates, that prayer rugs did not benefit from a similar munificence. The few prayer rugs which have been attributed to this period bear inscriptions, most of which are from the Koran (Erdmann 1941, p. 165, Abb. 7-9; Erdmann 1970, pp. 76-80; Beattie 1972, pp. 105-106).

In addition to the 17th century multiple-niche prayer rug fragment illustrated here, two other niches from what appears to be the same rug have been published (p. 133, Fig. 25) (Mann, pl. 119, color). The variation in the designs patterning the niches and the alternation in ground colors of dark blue and medium blue in this fragment also occur in multiple-niche prayer rugs from other rug weaving areas. Both the pattern in the upper niche and that in the spandrels of all four niches have been adopted from large rugs; neither fits its allotted space to maximum advantage. Composed of a combination of primary and secondary floral and foliate design systems, these patterns have an international Islamic court flavor characteristic of some 16th-17th century Ottoman, Safavid and Mughal art. The pattern in the lower niche, however, is considerably less international, especially in its representation on rugs. Small isolated plants with three blossoms are arranged in staggered rows. While similar small motifs pattern 17th century Persian silks, contemporary rugs with comparable patterns are not known. Isolated flowering plants achieved their greatest popularity in 17th century Mughal India in all media (larger scale, Dimand 1973, p. 151, fig. 134, color). The particular color tones and their combination in this rug are also associated with Mughal weaving. This rug is firmly attributed by Ellis to Indian manufacture on the basis of its style, color and construction (unpublished).

Size: L. 2.31m (7'7'') (warp) × W. 1.01m (3'4'') (weft).

Warp: cotton, ivory, 6 Z-yarns S-plied, alternate warps very depressed.

Weft: cotton, ivory, 2 Z-yarns, 3 shots.

Pile: wool, 2 and 3 Z-yarns, Senneh knot open on the left, 13.5 horiz. × 18 vert. per in. (243 per sq. in.).

Color: 6, dark blue, light blue, blue-green, barn red, rose, ivory.

Condition: extensive reknotting throughout (some fugitive dyes used), border on right side is mostly original, cut down on all 4 sides.

Published: Dimand 1973, no. 50, fig. 123; Bode & Kühnel, fig. 116; Breck & Morris, no. 11.

XXVI

XXVII
Persia or probably India, Kashmir Area, late 18th century

Loaned by The Fogg Art Museum, Harvard University, Cambridge, Mass., on loan from the Joseph V. McMullan Estate

The luxuriantly blossoming field of this prayer rug has caused its pattern to be called *mille-fleurs*. A symmetrical, chimerical floral display grows from a vase, placed above a shallow bowl on a hillock. Various isolated blossoming plants appear on and above the hillock. Large half cypress trees flank the field suggesting columns, especially in the fanciful treatment of their trunks. Lush floral growth also patterns the spandrels and main border, whose lower corners are skillfully turned. This particular prayer rug is an especially fine example of this group which is often characterized by stiff drawing and crowded compositions (McMullan, pls. 30, color, & 32). The provenance of these rugs has been controversial (Ettinghausen 1970, pl. 16, calls this rug "Mughal"; Ellis 1969, p. 19, calls it "Indian"). Their prototype, which is generally attributed to 17th century Mughal manufacture, displays graceful and spacious drawing with beautiful coloration (p. 133, Fig. 24) (Schlosser, pl. 86, color; Sarre & Trenkwald, vol. I, pl. 37, color). Beattie has pointed out that the *mille-fleurs* rugs and the 17th century

Mughal prayer rugs have several distinctive technical features in common which further substantiates the attribution of the *mille-fleurs* prayer rugs to India, possibly to the area of Kashmir (Beattie 1972, p. 67).

Analysis courtesy of Charles Grant Ellis.
Size: L. 1.73m (5'8'') × W. 1.067m (3'6'').
Warp: silk, bands of red, yellow, pale blue, ivory, 2 Z-yarns S-plied, alternate warps very depressed.
Weft: cotton, beige, 2 Z-yarns, 3 shots.
Pile: pashm, multiple (as high as 7) Z-yarns, Senneh knot open on the left, 16 horiz. × 17 vert. per in. (272 per sq. in.).
Color: (incomplete), yellow, red, very dark blue, dark blue, medium blue, blue-green, ivory.
Condition: woven bottom end first, ends: light yellow silk then light blue silk, weft-faced plain weave; no original selvedges.
Published: Ettinghausen 1970, pl. 16; Ellis 1969, fig. 28; McMullan, pl. 31, color.

XXVII

XXVIII
Tapestry-Woven Rug or Kilim, Senneh, 19th century
Loaned by Jerome A. Straka

Tapestry-woven or kilim prayer rugs woven in Senneh are probably the best known Persian prayer rugs. They are characterized by a boldly outlined niche with deep indentations in the profile of the arch. The actual shape of the arch seems to vary considerably (McMullan, pls. 35 & 36, color). Frequently, one floral motif arranged in staggered rows patterns both the field of the niche and that of the spandrels. The drawing is generally angular. The Senneh kilim illustrated here displays an alternate layout in which the niche is divided into narrow stripes with seven different ground colors. The curvilinear drawing which characterizes this very fine prayer kilim is atypical and indicates skilled weaving. Alternate stripes are patterned by variously colored, isolated, flowering plants. The interstitial stripes display four types of continuous flowering vine motifs. The floral decoration in the spandrels is surprisingly naturalistic. The main border pattern displays a continuous vine bearing blue and red blossoms and green leaves. More stylized renditions of this pattern frequently fill the main border of these kilims.

All the stripes in the niche and the several narrow monochrome guard stripes have a stepped outline which is a handsome solution to what would otherwise be a technical problem. Since these rugs are slit tapestry, each colored weft is worked only in the specific area where it is needed with "no structural connection between laterally adjacent areas" of different colors (Emery, p. 79). The stepped outline therefore minimizes the length of each slit; a straight outline would obviously produce a slit the entire length of the stripe.

Size: L. 1.635m (5'4¼") × W. 1.194m (3'11").
Warp: wool, ivory, 4 Z-yarns S-plied.
Weft: wool, 2 Z-yarns S-plied, slit tapestry.
Color: 13, maroon, red, pale red, tan, brown, dark brown, very dark blue, medium blue, blue-green, green, light green, yellow, ivory.
Condition: woven bottom end first, cut lengthwise 2 stripes to right of center where 1 stripe is missing, numerous small repairs, ends: 1 row weft twining, 1 row of warp braiding, knotted warp fringe; selvedges: red wool.
Unpublished.

XXVIII

CAUCASIAN PRAYER RUGS

The Caucasus, the mountainous region lying between the Black Sea and the Caspian, is peopled by Armenians, Georgians, tribes of Iranian and Turkish origin, and nomadic Tartars. At an early period, the Caucasus was subject to cultural and artistic influences from Persia and from nomadic Scythians and Sarmatians. The conquest of some parts of the Caucasus by the Arabs was gradual. By the middle of the eleventh century, only Derbent, in the Province of Dagestan, was in Muslim hands. In 1049, the Turkish Seljuks invaded Armenia, Georgia and other parts of the Caucasus, including Dagestan.

The rugs, including prayer rugs, of the Caucasus were made by peasants and nomads and can be divided into several groups, with features peculiar to various regions and provinces. The earliest Caucasian rugs known to us are the so-called Dragon rugs. There has been a considerable difference of opinion about the provenance and dating of these rugs. Some authors, as for instance, F. R. Martin, dated them as early as the thirteenth century. Other writers assigned them to the fourteenth and fifteenth centuries. It is now definitely established that early Dragon rugs cannot be much earlier than the end of the sixteenth century. The later ones range in date from the seventeenth to the nineteenth centuries. The Dragon rugs were for a long time attributed to Armenia and, therefore, called Armenian. This theory was challenged by Heinrich Jacoby and Arthur Upham Pope, who rightly assigned these rugs to the region of Kuba in the eastern Caucasus. The province of Kuba is populated both by Armenians and Turks. Both produced Dragon rugs and related floral rugs with large palmettes derived from Persian rugs.

During the nineteenth century, several types of Caucasian rugs were made in various regions and provinces. Among the main types are Kubas, the Shirvans, Dagestans, Lesghians, Chichis, Bakus, Talish, Moghan, Karabaghs, and Kazaks. In all these regions, the natives produced highly decorative prayer rugs which show different patterns, characteristic of the regions.

Among the well-known prayer rugs are those made in the Shirvan district. Several of them with a pattern of stylized palmettes are sometimes attributed to Kuba, but were most probably made in northern Shirvan. Some of them are dated: one in a private collection in New York is dated 1861. The palmettes are arranged in staggered rows and rendered in vivid colors. The borders show the "crab" motif, which appears in some Kazaks. Although without mihrabs, these small rugs should also be regarded as prayer rugs.

Another type of Shirvan prayer rug is sometimes attributed to the village of Marasali. The field, sometimes blue, has an angular arch, and is filled with rows of cone-shaped palmettes, containing various geometrical designs. Such a prayer rug in the Metropolitan Museum is dated 1808/09.

North of Kuba lies the district of Dagestan, which produced fine textured rugs with a pattern of stylized flowers. Among them are prayer rugs with an angular mihrab, usually on a white ground. The whole field has a lozenge diaper, filled with stylized blossoms. The borders usually have a series of angular S-motifs. Some of them bear dates as late as 1867.

Northwest of Dagestan is the district of Lesghistan, where prayer rugs similar to the Dagestans were made. The design consists of boldly stylized blossoms but rendered in brighter colors on white, yellow or blue ground.

The Kazak district, in southwestern Caucasus, also produced prayer rugs which in many ways resemble the regular rugs made by the nomads. They show bold geometrical motifs in rich colors typical of the Kazaks. To the village of Fachralo are attributed prayer rugs with a prayer niche in red, containing a polygon and other geometrical motifs. M.S.D.

XXIX
Shirvan, early 19th century
Loaned by Jerome A. Straka

Among the several known examples of this specific pattern, the superb juxtaposition of colors, detailed drawing, and lustrous quality of the wool must qualify this rug as one of the finest of its type. The keel-shaped arch appears to interrupt the all over pattern of rows of cone-shaped *buti* (botehs) facing in alternate directions. A wealth of linear motifs patterns the *buti* which are silhouetted by a jagged outline on the rich blue ground. The beauty of the rug is greatly enriched and enlivened by the random use of colors and designs on each *buta*. On less fine examples which may have been woven somewhat later, all the *buti* face in one direction and the combination of color and linear design is often organized on an obvious diagonal (e.g., Schürmann n.d., pl. 78, color). While the exact origin of the *buta* remains unclear, it appears to have developed from a stylization of 17th century Persian isolated blossoming plants. It was widely used in many media in India and Persia, and on rugs in Persia and the Caucasus. The combination of border patterns on this rug is characteristic of this specific group. The most distinctive although un-identifiable pattern is that of the main border which also defines the arch of the niche. It is possibly another rendition of a *buta*. Flanking the main bor-

94

der are floral and reciprocally-patterned guard stripes.

A somewhat comparable rug in the Metropolitan Museum of Art is dated the equivalent of 1808-09 (Dimand 1973, fig. 237). Although the exact provenance of these rugs remains uncertain, it is clear that they are among the most finely woven rugs from the Caucasus. This rug has about 287 knots per square inch.

Size: L. 1.143m (3'9'') × W. 0.889m (2'11'').
Warp: wool, ivory, 4 Z-yarns S-plied.
Weft: wool, Z-yarns, 2 shots.
Pile: wool, 2 Z-yarns, Gördes knot, 12.5 horiz. × 23 vert. per in. (287.5 per sq. in.).
Color: 9, dark blue, medium blue, maroon, brownish-red, brown, mustard, blue-green, greenish-tan, ivory.
Condition: woven bottom end first, few small tears, no original ends or selvedges.
Published: *Fortune,* May, 1968, p. 165, illus.; *Katalog Wystawy Kobiercow Mahometanskich Ceramiki Azjatyckiej i Europejskiej* (Catalogue National Museum in Krakow), Krakowie, 1934, cat. no. 38, illus. under no. 41.

XXIX

XXX
Multiple-Niche Prayer Rug or Saff,
Dagestan or Shirvan,
dated H. 1292/1875 A.D.
Loaned by Frank M. Michaelian

The extreme scarcity of multiple-niche prayer rugs from the Caucasus greatly enhances the importance of this rug. Although one diamond motif patterns six of the seven niches, the variation in ground color, deep blue, yellow and ivory, and the rich varied coloring of the diamonds, create a rhythm which partially disguises the otherwise repetitive nature of the pattern. Each silhouetted diamond is subdivided into four squares with the colors organized on diagonal lines. The one diagonally striped niche adds an element of surprise and reminds us of the personal involvement in the weaving of each of these rugs. A characteristic feature of Caucasian prayer rugs is the isolation of the band defining the arch and top of the niche; it does not continue to form the sides of the niche. The narrowness of the saw-tooth borders which separate the seven niches is noteworthy and contrasts with the wider borders of many Islamic multiple-niche prayer rugs. The main border pat-

tern, red *buti* (botehs) on an ivory ground, also appears on no. XXIX. The blue guard stripes display a meandering red vine and varied colored blossoms. An additional feature of this rug is that five of the seven niches are dated 1292 (1875 A.D.). Whether the rug was woven in Dagestan or Shirvan is a matter which awaits further investigation.

Size: L. 2.843m (9'4'') (warp) × W. 1.422m (4'8'') (weft).
Warp: wool, brown and white, Z-yarns S-plied.
Weft: cotton, ivory, S-yarns.
Pile: wool, 2 Z-yarns, Gördes knot, 9 horiz. × 9 vert. per in. (81 per sq. in.).
Color: 11, medium blue, light blue, medium green, light green, yellow, red, deep red, aubergine, tan, black, ivory.
Condition: good, original ends and selvedges.
Unpublished.

XXX

XXXI
Dagestan, dated H. 1311/1893-94 A.D.
Loaned by Charles Grant Ellis

Although large Caucasian rugs survive which are attributed to the 16th-17th century, prayer rugs either were not woven at that time or have not survived. Caucasian prayer rugs are not known to predate 1800. A surprisingly large number of these 19th century rugs bear dates that are usually based on the Islamic calendar (nos. XXX, XXXIII). Sometimes a date appears twice with one written forward and the other in mirror image; the date of 1311 is written backwards twice, however, on this rug.

The niche in the majority of Dagestan and Shirvan prayer rugs is filled by rows of a single motif; the use of color and smaller superimposed designs are major factors affecting the appearance of the motif. They can either disguise and thereby vitalize the pattern or through an organized arrangement emphasize its intrinsically repetitive nature. The coloring on this rug of the hooked diamonds containing octagons is arranged on what

becomes prominent diagonals. Small scattered diamonds, however, boast unpredictable color changes. The boldness and clarity of the drawing of these hooked diamonds are complemented by the isolated blossoms of the three patterned borders.

Size: L. 1.473m (4'10'') × W. 1.06m (3'5¾'').
Warp: wool, mixed browns, 3 Z-yarns S-plied.
Weft: cotton, ivory, 2 Z-yarns S-plied, 2 shots.
Pile: wool, 2 Z-yarns, Gördes knot, 8 horiz. × 10.5 vert. per in. (84 per sq. in.).
Color: 10, red, maroon, pale salmon, dark blue, medium blue, sea green, tan, mustard, brown-black, ivory.
Condition: woven bottom end first, patch upper center of niche, few small holes, 1 end: ivory cotton, weft-faced plain weave; selvedges: ivory cotton, 2 cords of 2 warps.
Unpublished.

98

XXXI

XXXII
Chichi, dated H. 1297/1879-80 A.D.
Loaned by Dr. M. A. S. de Reinis

In a characteristic Caucasian manner, a keel-shaped arch has been superimposed on an all over field pattern. The simplistic arrangement of isolated motifs in horizontal rows is artfully disguised by a varying alternation of rows and by the frequent color changes in the motifs. This masterful treatment of the field pattern draws the viewer into an examination of the design in a desire to comprehend the nature of its assemblage. Although such involvement is often inspired by the sophistication and complexity of Islamic court art, it is less frequently aroused by the simpler traditional folk arts.

While the field pattern is one of several used in Chichi rugs, that of the main border is the identifying hallmark. It is composed of rosettes alternating with diagonal bars. A variety of patterns is found in the several guard stripes; this rug displays stepped octagons and a continuous zigzag. An Islamic

calendar date, 1297 (1879-80 A.D.), appears twice at the top of the field.

Size: L. 1.575m (5'2'') × W. 1.295m (4'3'').
Warp: wool, ivory and brown, some ivory, 2 Z-yarns S-plied, alternate warps slightly depressed.
Weft: cotton, some wool, some cotton and wool, ivory, 3 Z-yarns S-plied, 2 shots.
Pile: wool, 2 Z-yarns, Gördes knot, 10 horiz. × 13.5 vert. per in. (135 per sq. in.).
Color: 7, dark blue, medium blue, blue-green, red, mustard, dark brown, ivory.
Condition: woven top end first, very good, ends: ivory cotton and some wool, weft-faced plain weave, knotted warp fringe; selvedges: ivory cotton and wool, 1 cord of 2 warps.
Unpublished.

100

XXXII

XXXIII
Gendje, dated H. 1289/1872-73 A.D.
Loaned by Harold M. Keshishian

Rich colors in vibrant juxtaposition vitalize the patterning of this rug. The dominance of the ivory and deep blue diagonal bands, separated by polychromatic narrow stripes, is complemented by the random coloring of the square with its two rigid horizontal hooks. A characteristic Caucasian keel-shaped arch is surrounded by hooked motifs. The representation of a pair of hands beside the arch is found almost exclusively on Caucasian prayer rugs from many rug-weaving centers and on Beluch prayer rugs. They are traditionally associated with the placement of the faithful's hands during prayer. The location of the hands from a functional point of view, however, is too high; it would necessitate placing one's forehead off the top of the rug during prayer. Is another association more valid? Hands have long been represented throughout the Near East invoking a variety of divine and magical symbolic associations, some of which continued after the advent of Islam. Additional symbolism developed based on Koranic references to the hand of Allah, which can be associated with the magical number five, "derived from the five basic tenets of Islam, the five daily prayers, and the five members of the Prophet's family, i.e. Muhammad, Ali, Fatimah, Hasan, and Husain" (Ettinghausen 1954,

p. 151; see also Cammann, pp. 20, 21). Whether this specific religious symbolism was intended on Caucasian prayer rugs awaits verification.

The pattern of the central border displays star-shaped rosettes alternating with diagonal bars. The flanking borders contain one pattern, that of squares bearing swastikas with short vines and three leaves. The date of the rug appears in the arch: 1289 (1872-73 A.D.).

Size: L. 1.78m (5'10'') × W. 1.034m (3'4½'').
Warp: wool, ivory, 3 Z-yarns S-plied.
Weft: cotton, ivory, 2 Z-yarns S-plied, 2-4 shots.
Pile: wool, 2 Z-yarns, Gördes knot, 7.5 horiz. × 8.5 vert. per in. (63.75 per sq. in.).
Color: 15, deep blue, medium blue, aqua, wine-red, rose, coral, medium green, yellow, tan, brown, brown-black, purple, 2 fugitive dyes from shades of purple, ivory.
Condition: woven bottom end first, small hole upper right corner, several fugitive dyes, ends: ivory cotton, weft-faced plain weave, 2 rows of warp braiding, knotted warp fringe; selvedges: varying colors of wool, 3 cords of 2 warps, attached by ground weft around inner warp of outer cord.
Unpublished.

XXXIII

XXXIV
Kazak, 19th century
Loaned by Karl F. Milde

More variation occurs in the definition of the niche in Kazak prayer rugs than in other types of Caucasian prayer rugs. While a number of Kazaks have the typical Caucasian isolated band forming only the arch and top of the niche (Tschebull, pl. 11), many Kazaks display the outline of the entire niche which appears as a self-contained unit on the rectangular field of the rug (Tschebull, pls. 9, 10, 12). Many also have a rectangular indentation at the bottom of the niche.

This rug displays a variation of the above with one blue band serving as both the outline of the niche and the inner guard stripe. Although one large medallion may more commonly pattern the niche's field on Kazak rugs, the strongly drawn motifs seen here and their combination, together with their coloring, form a striking and powerful ensemble. The main border pattern is a stylized rendition of a serrated leaf alternating with a tulip. The varied coloring not only breaks up the pattern but denies it continuity. This pattern is not limited to use on Caucasian rugs; it sometimes forms the main borders of earlier Anatolian rugs (McMullan, nos. 98, 99) which may have served as the design source for this border in Caucasian rugs. A similar influence may have affected the portrayal of the niche. The representation of a self-contained niche including the indentation at the bottom of its field,

which typifies many Kazaks, is not common in Turkish prayer rugs but characterizes one group (nos. VIII, IX) datable as early as the 16th century. It is not known whether there was direct influence, whether the two developed from a common source, or whether the similar portrayal is merely fortuitous.

[The oblong panel at the bottom of the field probably is a degeneration of the mountain form found in a similar position in the Mamluk prayer rug which survives and in a number of Turkish examples of greater age than the Kazak rugs, as mentioned. C. G. Ellis]

Analysis courtesy of Raoul Tschebull.
Size: L. 1.60m (5'3'') × W. 1.245m (4'1'').
Warp: wool, ivory, 3 Z-yarns S-plied.
Weft: wool, red, 2 Z-yarns S-plied, 2-4 (mostly 3) shots.
Pile: wool, 2 Z-strands, Gördes knot, 6-8 horiz. × 6.5-8 vert. per in. (39-64 per sq. in.).
Color: 6, red, royal blue, yellow, light green, dark brown, ivory.
Condition: good, no original ends, selvedges: red wool, 2 cords of 2 warps.
Published: Tschebull, pl. 18, color.

104

XXXIV

TURKOMAN PRAYER RUGS

During the nineteenth century, the wandering Turkoman tribes of Western or Russian Turkestan occupied the region stretching from the Caspian Sea eastward to Bukhara, northward to the Aral Sea, and southward to Persia, including Afghanistan and areas of Beluchistan. These tribes were skilled weavers of rugs, which served as floor coverings for their tents, as hangings for the tent entrances, as tent bags, saddle bags, and prayer rugs. Although all the Turkoman rugs have common characteristics, each tribe developed its own peculiar ornament and distinctive tribal "gul" or flower. The names of the various Turkoman tribes are used to designate the main types of rugs: Tekke, Salor, Saryk, Yomud, Ersari, Afghan and Beluchistan. The patterns of these rugs are mostly geometrical, but also floral or animal stylized in geometrical fashion. The predominant color ranges from a reddish brown to a dark brown; additional colors, usually few in number, are mainly shades of blue, green, orange and yellow. The Turkoman rugs show either the Ghiordes or Senna knot.

A number of rugs which are often referred to as prayer rugs (namazlik) have a cross composition (hatchli) in the field which is divided into four rectangular sections. In the opinion of some experts on Turkoman rugs, these rugs were used more often as entrance rugs (engsi) of the tents. Such rugs were made by several tribes, such as Salor, Saryk, Tekke, Ersari, Yomud and Afghan.

Among the most beautiful Turkoman prayer rugs or door rugs are those made by the Saryk tribe, chiefly in the oasis of Pinde. They show a mosaic-like pattern. The central field has two mihrabs or prayer niches separated by a horizontal band, with a geometrical pattern, and a lozenge diaper with hooks, as seen in a rug formerly in the collection of Amos B. Thacher, in which mahogany brown is the predominant color. The mihrabs contain the tree of life motif and are flanked at each side by a Kufic-like ornament ending in heads of stylized birds. The same "bird" motif appears in two vertical bands of the inner border and in a horizontal band below the niches. The upper cross panel has a row of nine angular niches, while the lower cross panel has a row of devices with peculiar comb or hand motifs. The Pinde rugs have borders divided into several narrow bands with a variety of geometrical motifs, among them the angular hook and the "comb" motifs.

The clans of the Ersari tribe, occupying the territory on both sides of the Oxus River, northward from Afghanistan to the city of Bukhara, produced several types of rugs, including prayer rugs. Some of the Ersaris are known in the trade as "Beshirs." The Ersari branch of the southern region, the Kizil Ayak clan, often used the motifs of their neighbors, the Saryks. Further north in the Bukhara region, the Ersari weavers were influenced by the designs of the Persian rugs. Fine examples of Ersari prayer rugs are in some private collections. The field has an outer large niche and an inner smaller one, decorated with vertical rows of pomegranates, which appear also in the spandrels. The color scheme is richer than in other Turkoman rugs: reddish brown, creamy white, yellow and deep blue.

Prayer rugs were also made by the Beluchi or Beluchistan tribes occupying various parts of southern Afghanistan and adjoining areas of Persia or Iran. Some of the prayer rugs attributed to Beluchis show rich colors with a tree of life within the niche of the field. The branches of the tree bear stylized blossoms, resembling carnations. The blues and reds of the pattern are deep and brilliant against a background of natural camel's hair.   M.S.D.

XXXV
Door Rug or Prayer Rug, Saryk,
19th century
From the collection of Amos B. Thacher

Clear drawing and deep rich colors, especially a radiant mahogany red, characterize fine old Saryks of which this is a classic example. The origin of the layout and design motifs has been lost because the utilitarian function of Turkoman rugs minimized their chances for long survival. This accounts for the fact that they rarely if ever predate the 19th century. Additionally, the Turkomans' nomadic life style kept their rugs from being housed in mosques or other public buildings which have preserved old rugs in other areas.

The cross layout, referred to as *hatchli*, in the center of the field characterizes a series of rugs of similar size made by several Turkoman tribes (nos. XXXVI, XXXVII) and precludes the use of the tribe's identifying octagonal "gul." Two arches appear on the central axis, one above the other, displaying what is believed to be a stylized tree. Angular renditions of flora also pattern the border areas. A characteristic feature of many Turkoman border stripes occurs in exaggeration on Saryk prayer rugs; few of them retain the same width or design on all four sides of the rug with the result that the field and border areas visually interact. The horizontal panel near the top of the rug composed of adjacent forms, possibly arches, is also an identify-ing feature. The continuous band outlining these forms sometimes provides space between them (Schürmann 1969, pls. 36, 37) in a manner highly reminiscent of the crenelated frieze seen on several types of Turkish prayer rugs (nos. I, XII, XVI, XIX). Whether this is a fortuitous parallel, the result of direct influence, or the two developed from a common and now lost source remains unknown.

Technical data derived primarily from an analysis by Amos B. Thacher.
Size: L. 1.778m (5'10'') × W. 1.245m (4'1'').
Warp: wool or goat hair (?), ivory, 2 Z-yarns S-plied, alternate warps slightly depressed.
Weft: wool, mixed light browns, I-yarns, 2 shots.
Pile: wool (polychrome) and goat hair (?) (mixed dark browns), 2 Z-yarns and 3 Z-yarns, cotton, 2 Z-yarns and 3 Z-yarns (ivory), Gördes knot (slant to left), 10 horiz. × 16 vert. per in. (160 per sq. in.).
Color: 7, mahogany red, rose, orange-red, light orange-red, dark blue, brown, ivory.
Condition: woven bottom end first, few scattered repairs especially upper right and upper left corners, no original ends or selvedges.
Published: Thacher, pl. 9; Dimand 1961, no. 31, illus. p. 37.

XXXV

XXXVI
Door Rug or Prayer Rug, Tekke,
late 19th century
The Textile Museum, R 37.1.4

Tekke door or prayer rugs utilize the popular Turkoman *hatchli* or cross layout, the prototype of which has been lost. Two niches, which are atypically narrow on this rug, appear on the central axis. Above them is a characteristically pronounced arch. The Y-shaped forms which flank the niches are identifying motifs on these Tekke rugs. Although several of the border stripes do not continue on all four sides of the rug, especially along the bottom, the typical and widest border pattern is continuous. Its serrated diagonal lines have been derived from stylized renditions of plants which are readily recognizable on some Tekke rugs of this type. The random coloring of the serrated lines enlivens and shrouds the otherwise repetitive nature of the pattern. The design elements of the outer border and bottom apron are also typical of these rugs. The colors of

rich red, deep blue and browns, the sheen of the wool, and the very supple nature of this rug are characteristic of 19th century Tekkes.

Size: L. 1.55m (5'1'') × W. 1.232m (4'1½'').
Warp: wool or goat hair (?), Z-yarns S-plied.
Weft: wool or goat hair (?), tan to brown, 2 Z-yarns, 2 shots.
Pile: wool, 2 Z-yarns, Senneh knot open on the right (2 Gördes knots at each end of each row), 9 horiz. × 16 vert. per in. (144 per sq. in.).
Color: 5, maroon, salmon, deep blue, brown, ivory.
Condition: woven top end first, 1 repaired hole, no original ends; selvedges: deep blue wool, 1 cord of 2 warps, attached by ground weft around both warps.
Unpublished.

110

XXXVI

XXXVII
Door Rug or Prayer Rug, Afghan,
late 19th century

The Textile Museum, Gift of Bernard B. Lieder,
1972.26.45

While the rugs of many Turkoman tribes are finely woven with relatively refined patterning, those woven by the Afghans sometimes appear in comparison to be both visually and technically coarse. Bold, stark motifs generally pattern these rugs however, and often create a strong *tour de force*. The Afghans' handling of the *hatchli* or cross layout is noticeably different from its representation by other Turkoman tribes (cf. nos. XXXV and XXXVI). With a more spacious drawing of boldly rendered motifs, the Afghans display the typical two niches, one above the other on the central axis, flanked by an angular linear motif. In contrast to the Tekke and in particular the Saryk *hatchli* rugs, the border stripes on the Afghans generally continue around all four sides of the rug. An end apron at the bottom of the rug often displays floral motifs, either plants or blossoms as

seen here. Of all the rugs which use the *hatchli* plan, those woven by the Afghans are undoubtedly the scarcest in the Western world.

Size: L. 1.702m (5'7'') × W. 1.422m (4'8'').
Warp: wool or goat hair (?), mixed browns, 2 Z-yarns S-plied.
Weft: wool, brown, Z-yarns, 2 shots.
Pile: wool, 2 Z-yarns, Senneh knot open on the right, 8 horiz. × 8 vert. per in. (64 per sq. in.).
Color: 7, red, deep orange, very dark blue, royal blue, brown, tan, ivory.
Condition: woven bottom end first, good, ends: stripes of red, royal blue and brown, weft-faced plain weave (long apron at bottom, top turned under); selvedges: brown, coarse wool (?), 3 cords of 3 warps.
Unpublished.

XXXVII

XXXVIII
Prayer Rug, Chodor, 19th century
Loaned by Jerome A. Straka

Both the lighter palette and the "gul" patterned field are striking features of this rare Chodor prayer rug. Two arches, one inside the other, are set at the top of the field and extend into the end apron. Although well drawn and balanced, they appear superimposed on a field of what otherwise would have been a regular Chodor rug. The Chodor "gul," a stepped octagon with a symmetrical hook extending from its top and bottom, is characteristically arranged in staggered rows. The identically drawn "guls" benefit from varied although predictable color alternations which greatly enliven the rhythm of the field. While this is one of several closely related "gul" patterns used in Chodor rugs, the secondary pattern may be even more immediately identifying. It is composed of a jagged lattice displaying small rosettes which frames each "gul." The main border pattern, which is slightly compressed across the ends of the rug, provides a good balance for the pattern of the field and is further complemented by the end aprons whose stepped lozenges are vibrantly colored on diagonals which form bold chevrons.

Size: L. 1.83m (6') × W. 1.07m (3'6").
Warp: wool, mixed browns with some ivory, 2 Z-yarns S-plied.
Weft: wool, mixed browns with some ivory, 2 Z-yarns, 2 shots.
Pile: wool, 2 Z-yarns, Senneh knot open on the right, 7 horiz. × 13 vert. per in. (91 per sq. in.).
Color: 6, red, purple, blue-green, dark brown, tan, ivory.
Condition: woven bottom end first, some worn areas, no original ends, selvedges: coarse brown wool (?), 4 cord, attached by ground weft around inside cord.
Published: Reed, cat. no. 37, illus.; Schürmann 1969, pl. 14, color.

XXXVIII

XXXIX
Prayer Rug, Ersari, 19th century
The Textile Museum, Bequest of Arthur J. Arwine,
1968.18.2

From the rug-weaving tribe of Ersari whose large population spread over wide areas, those living in the area of Bukhara, a former center of Islamic culture and civilization, wove highly distinctive prayer rugs. Their prayer rugs contrast with most Turkoman prayer rugs not only in the profile of their niche but also in their brighter palette with its extensive use of ivory wool. The shape of the niche is peculiar to the Ersari tribe who typically display one niche within another. The niche's profile, which is not known to be indigenous to the region, caused Thacher to speculate on whether a common source might have existed for this and the Turkish Milas prayer rugs (Thacher, p. 28), whose dependence on earlier models has already been cited (no. XX). The ivory area typically forms the major portion of the niche on which a lush growth of pomegranates is displayed. Although the more naturalistic representation of the plants on the red ground of the inscribed niche and on the spandrels is an unusual feature in other Turkoman rugs, it is characteristic of Ersari weaving. The ivory ground of the reciprocally-patterned guard stripe outlining the spandrels is skillfully harmonized with the strong visual impact of the niche. The same reciprocal pattern also occurs in the yellow ground of the

outer guard stripe. An extension of the main border is frequently used to define the profile of the red niche within the ivory niche. An extremely similar rug is illustrated by Schürmann 1969, pl. 48 (color).

Size: L. 1.67m (5'5½'') × W. 1.03m (3'4½'').
Warp: wool and goat hair (?), ivory with some brown added, 2 Z-yarns S-plied.
Weft: wool, pale red, 2 Z-yarns S-plied (very loose), 2 shots.
Pile: wool, 2 Z-yarns, Senneh knot open on the right, 7.5 horiz. × 11 vert. per in. (82.5 per sq. in.).
Color: 7, red, royal blue, dark blue, blue-green, mustard, brown-black, ivory.
Condition: woven bottom end first, brown-black disintegrating and partially replaced by medium brown (especially in border), occasional reknotting in fugitive colors now pea green and light green, ends: stripes of red, royal and dark blue wool, weft-faced plain weave (knotting of warp fringe not original); selvedges, royal blue wool, 2 cords of 2 warps.
Published: "Some Recent Acquisitions to the Textile Museum's Collections," *Textile Museum Journal*, Vol. II, No. 4 (1969), p. 45, fig. 1.

XXXIX

Full view of Ersari *saff.*

XL
Multiple-Niche Prayer Rug or Saff, Ersari, 19th century
Loaned by Jerome A. Straka

Multiple-niche prayer rugs woven by Tur-koman tribes are extremely rare. The distinctive shape of the niches on this rug is characteristic of that found on Ersari single-niche rugs. The ivory band which typically defines the niche displays an isolated motif, alternately in red and blue, which was also used to form part of the main border pattern on the single-niche prayer rug, no. XXXIX. Fanciful plants pattern the red ground within the niche and in the spandrels. The plants appear in the same location on each of the twelve niches but with slight color changes which partially disguise their repetitive nature. Although vertical stripes are suggested between the niches by the repetition of an "hour-glass" motif, the separation of the niches is visually minimized by the lack of a color change in the red ground of the adjacent spandrels and the suggested stripe. The large continuous pattern on the white ground of the main border is an unusual and noteworthy feature of this large rug.

Size: L. 6.71m (22') × W. 1.475m (4'10'').
Warp: coarse wool or goat hair (?), mixed browns, 2 Z-yarns S-plied.
Weft: wool, light red, 2 Z-yarns S-plied, 2 shots.
Pile: wool, 2 Z-yarns, Senneh knot open on the right (slant to right), 7 horiz. × 8 vert. per in. (56 per sq. in.).
Color: 6, red, blue, green, yellow, brown, ivory.
Condition: woven right end first, worn areas, ends: red wool, weft-faced plain weave; selvedges: brown wool (?), 3 cord.
Published: Jones 1969, cat. no. 1; *Fortune*, May, 1968, p. 165, illus.

118

XLI
Prayer Rug, Beluch, 19th century
Loaned by Alvin W. Pearson

The rugs woven by the Beluch, who are not of Turkoman origin, are usually discussed in conjunction with Turkoman rugs because of their affinity with these rugs. The older Beluch prayer rugs have a highly desirable identifying feature which may be peculiar to them: lustrous natural camel's hair provides a rich ground for patterning in very subtle shades of wine-red, maroon, dark blue, and dark brown. The three bands which outline the niche are particularly distinctive and possibly owe their origin to more western rugs, either from the Caucasus or Turkey. A clearly drawn tree dominates the field of the niche. Its leaves are quartered with opposing quadrants in the same color, a feature which is characteristic of the coloring of the identifying "guls" of several Turkoman tribes (e.g., Tekke, Saryk, Yomud). Together the drawing and coloring create a well balanced and harmonious design. The Arabic inscription, "Allah is most great" (the reading of the word for "most great" is tentative), is written backwards in the stepped octagon at the top of the tree. Similar octagons also pattern the two rectangles on either side of the arch. These rectangles sometimes display an alternate motif: a pair of

hands (see no. XXXIII). Two narrow guard stripes bearing a surprisingly delicate and accomplished reciprocal trefoil flank the main border whose directional pattern is highly stylized.

An additional feature of this classic Beluch prayer rug is the presence of silk pile. The strong yellow and mint green silk appear only in the two outer outline bands of the niche where they form diamonds and serve as accent dots.

Size: L. 1.422m (4'8") × W. 0.787m (2'7").
Warp: wool, ivory, 2 Z-yarns S-plied.
Weft: wool, dark brown, Z-yarns, 2 shots.
Pile: wool, 2 Z-yarns (wine-red, deep maroon, orange, navy blue, ivory); silk, Z-yarns (yellow, mint green); camel hair, 2 Z-yarns (natural camel hair); Senneh knot open on the left, 11.5 horiz. × 14 vert. per in. (161 per sq. in.).
Color: 9, wine-red, deep maroon, orange, navy blue, yellow, mint green, dark brown, camel hair, ivory.
Condition: woven bottom end first, very good, no original ends or selvedges.
Unpublished.

XLI

PRAYER RUGS
OF OTHER AREAS

Full view of Khotan *saff*.

XLII
Multiple-Niche Prayer Rug or Saff, Khotan, Chinese Turkestan, 19th century
Loaned by Jerome A. Straka

The location of Khotan on one of the main trade routes between the Islamic lands and China has made it a city of age-old importance. Khotan is believed to have served as the intermediary in relaying the guarded secret of sericulture to the Near East, and was described by a pilgrim during the T'ang period (618-906 A.D.) as having " 'fine woven silk fabrics, hair cloth of fine quality, and carpets' " (Mailey, p. 329). Among the various tribes from further north, east and west who ruled the area were those who professed the Muslim faith. One especially devout Muslim, Yaqub Beg (r. 1862-75) received honorific titles from the reigning Ottoman Sultan in Istanbul and rigorously enforced the observance of Islam.

It is noteworthy that the few prayer rugs which are attributed to Khotan all seem to have multiple-niches, usually numbering between five and twelve. The drawing of the niches displays considerable variation from rug to rug not only in the shape of the arch but also in the patterns within the niches. The illustrated eight-niche rug is a particularly handsome example of a well designed Khotan *saff*. The outline of these arches is dependent upon Chinese inspiration whereas the patterns within the niches are the result of local adaptations of western and eastern motifs. Both infinite and self-contained patterns appear on the varying ground colors of the niches and also in the spandrels. The main border pattern which is composed of blossoms and trilobed leaves also forms the vertical band between the individual niches.

Size: L. 4.37m (14'8'') (warp) × W. 1.092m (3'7'') (weft).
Warp: cotton, ivory, multiple Z-yarns S-plied.
Weft: wool, ivory, some brown, Z-yarns, 3 shots.
Pile: wool, 2 Z-yarns, Senneh knot open on the left, 5.5 horiz. × 5 vert. per in. (27.5 per sq. in.).
Color: 6, medium red, light salmon, deep blue, light blue, brown, ivory.
Condition: woven left end first, very good, minor wear along selvedges; ends: ivory, weft-faced plain weave; selvedges: red wool, 1 cord.
Published: *Christie's Review of the Season,* 1973, p. 399, illus.; *Christie's Forthcoming Sales,* Nov.-Dec. 1972, Thurs. Nov. 30, detail illus.; *Christie's Objects of Art and Clocks, Fine French and Continental Furniture, Tapestries, Eastern Rugs and Carpets,* Thurs. Nov. 30, 1972, cat. no. 155, pl. 42, detail.

124

XLIII
al-Fakihah, Lebanon,
19th-early 20th century
Loaned by Dr. and Mrs. Murray L. Eiland

The proximity of Lebanon to the very active rug producing countries of Turkey and Persia has prompted the development of several scattered rug manufactories within Lebanon during the last century. In the village of al-Fakihah, located in the valley of al-Biqa' in Lebanon, rugs similar to the illustrated example are still being woven (Nicolas Sursock Museum, p. 24, not paginated, pl. 86, written "Fikeh" and "Fikie"). The scale and proportions of the three "arches," which may possibly have evolved from Turkish triple-arch prayer rugs, greatly enhance the visual appearance of the rug. Small isolated geometric motifs appear at random in the magenta field of the niche and throughout the blue-green spandrels. The two border patterns are also composed of the repetition of individual motifs on magenta and dark blue grounds.

Size: L. 1.704m (5'11'') × W. 1.143m (3'9'').
Warp: wool, natural browns with some ivory, 2 Z-yarns S-plied.
Weft: wool, dark brown, Z-yarns, 2 shots.
Pile: wool, 2 Z-yarns, Gördes knot, 7 horiz. × 7 vert. per in. (49 per sq. in.).
Color: 11, magenta, bright orange, medium orange, pale orange, yellow, dark blue, medium blue, blue-green, brown, brown-black, ivory.
Condition: woven top end first, considerable re-knotting especially along central axis of rug, brown-black mostly disintegrated and partially replaced by dark brown, no original ends or selvedges.
Unpublished.

XLIII

RELATED
ILLUSTRATIONS

Figure 18—Detail of *miḥrab* with depiction of hanging lamp, 2 candlesticks, vase with varied flowers, arabesque patterned spandrels, Koranic inscriptions in cartouche, horizontal panel above with curved crenelations. Photograph courtesy Walter B. Denny (Denny, p. 12).

Figure 17—Ceramic tile *miḥrab* in the Green Mausoleum of Mehmet I, about 1421, Bursa. Courtesy Sonia P. & Hans C. Seherr-Thoss, *Design and Color in Islamic Architecture*, Washington, D.C., 1968, pl. 123.

129

Figure 20—Ottoman Court Manufactory prayer rug, Bursa (?), late 16th century, silk warp and weft. Islamic Museum, East Berlin, 89, 156. Courtesy Islamic Museum, East Berlin (see Ellis 1969, pp. 5-7).

Figure 19—Mamluk prayer rug, Cairo, *ca.* 1500. Islamic Museum, East Berlin, 88, 30. Courtesy Islamic Museum, East Berlin (see Enderlein; Ellis 1969, pp. 5-7).

Figure 21—Anatolian triple-arch prayer rug (see no. XII) in *Still Life* by Nicolaes van Gelder, 1664. Rijks Museum, Amsterdam. Courtesy Rijks Museum.

Figure 23—Mughal Indian prayer rug, probably a *saff* fragment, 17th century, approximately 1085 woolen Senneh knots per square inch. Thyssen-Bornemisza Collection. Courtesy Thyssen-Bornemisza Collection (see Beattie 1972, pp. 67-72, pl. IX, color).

Figure 22—Mughal Indian prayer rug, 17th century, approximately 2000 woolen Senneh knots per square inch. Jean Pincket Collection. Courtesy Jean Pinckett (see Ellis 1969, p. 18).

Figure 25—*Saff* fragment probably from the same rug as no. XXVI. After Kendrick & Tattersall, pl. 30B.

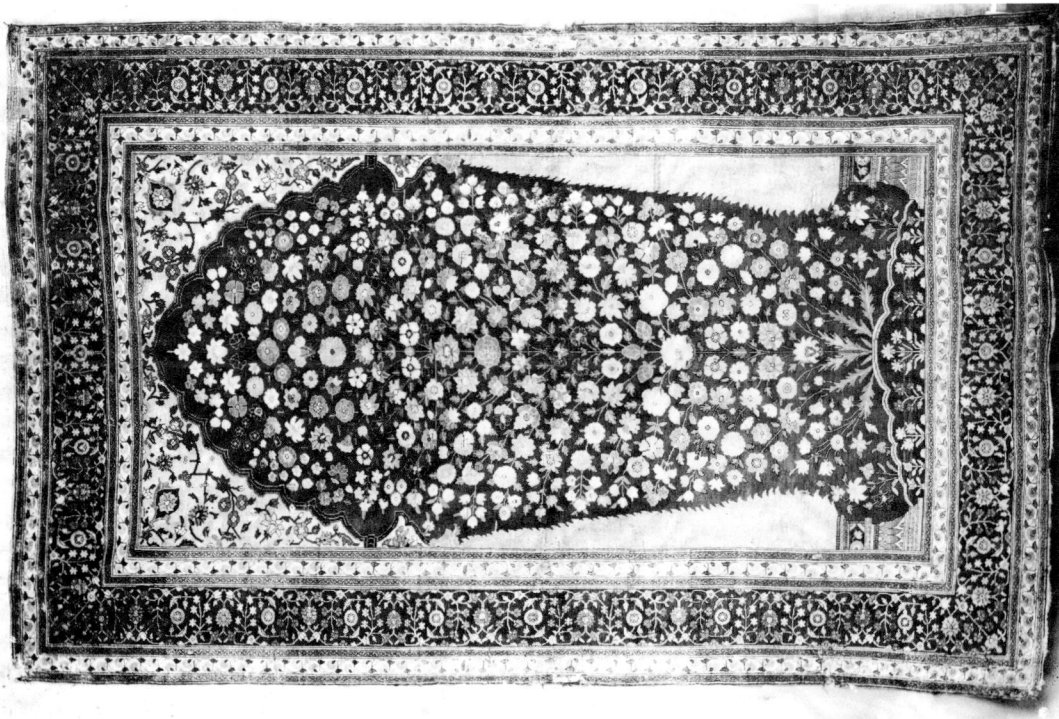

Figure 24 – Mughal India prayer rug with *mille-fleurs* pattern, 17th century. Museum of Decorative Art, Vienna, T 1539. Courtesy Museum of Decorative Art.

133

DEFINITIONS &
EXPLANATIONS

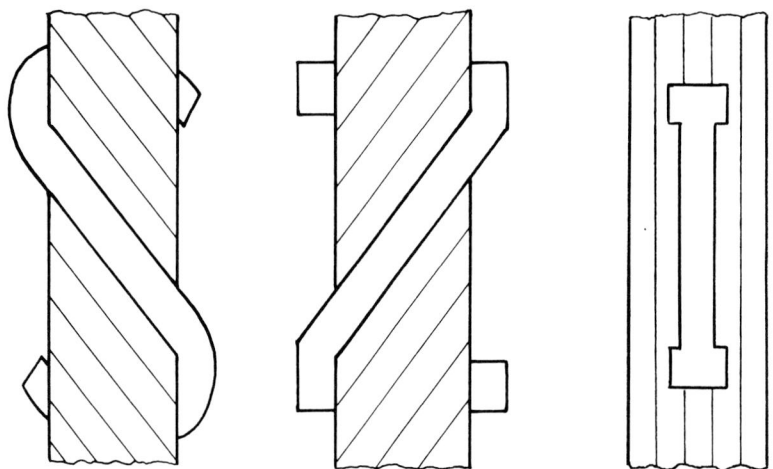

Figure 26–S-twist
Courtesy I. Emery

Z-twist
Courtesy I. Emery

I-"twist"
R. L. Fisher

S and Z   The direction of the spin or twist of a yarn conforms, when viewed in a vertical position, to the diagonal of the letter S or the letter Z.

I   When there is no apparent twist in the yarn, its fibers conform to the vertical of the letter I.

ply   The twisting together of two or more single yarns. The direction of ply is always apparent, while the direction of the original spin of the single yarns may be more difficult to determine. The direction of plying is usually opposite to the direction of the spin of the single yarns.

134

warp	Yarns that run lengthwise in a fabric from one end to the other, interlaced at right angles by the wefts, and around which the pile rug knots are wrapped. The warps in rugs are usually tightly spun and plied for strength.
weft	Yarns that run crosswise in a fabric from selvedge to selvedge, interlacing the warp at right angles. Unlike rug warps, rug wefts are often somewhat loosely spun and frequently not plied or very loosely plied. This allows the wefts to be firmly compacted and hold the rug knots securely in place.
shot	The passage of a weft across a fabric. In rugs, one or more weft shots, usually in plain weave, follow each horizontal row of knots.
pile	Yarns which project from the plane of a fabric to form a raised surface. The pile in rugs is composed of the cut ends (or loops) of the yarns which form the rug knots.

rug knots

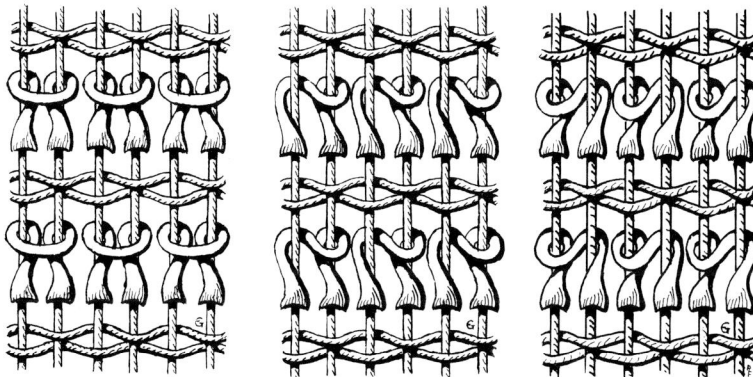

Figure 27—Gördes (Ghirodes) or "Turkish" symmetrical
Courtesy C.G. Ellis

Senneh or "Persian" asymmetrical, open on the left
Courtesy C.G. Ellis

Senneh or "Persian" asymmetrical, open on the right
R. L. Fisher

weft-faced plain weave	In plain weave, each weft passes alternately over and under successive warps producing the simplest possible interlacing of warp and weft elements. In weft-faced plain weave, the wefts are sufficiently numerous and compacted to cover the warps completely.
kilim	Tapestry-woven rug. Discontinuous colored wefts are woven back and forth in each color area in weft-faced plain weave. Rug specialists refer to kilims as flat-woven rugs to distinguish them from pile rugs.

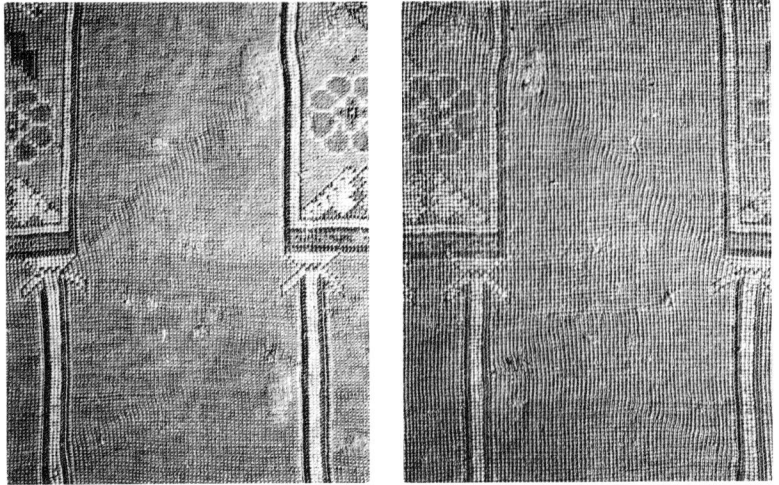

Figure 28—Lazy lines, detail of *back* of rug. (no. XIII)

Lazy lines, detail of same area on *front*.

lazy lines Diagonal lines, often several inches in length, formed by the meeting points of successive rows of discontinuous wefts of the same color. The discontinuous wefts replace the usually continuous wefts. In pile rugs, such lines are clearly visible on the back and on the upper surface if it is sufficiently worn.

Figure 29—A *saff* on a portable Bunyan loom in Kayseri, Turkey. Photograph courtesy May H. Beattie (Beattie 1963, pp. 6,7).

saff Arabic word for a multiple-niche prayer rug. The pattern of most *saffs* is woven sideways on the loom with the warps parallel to the longer dimension of the rug.

136

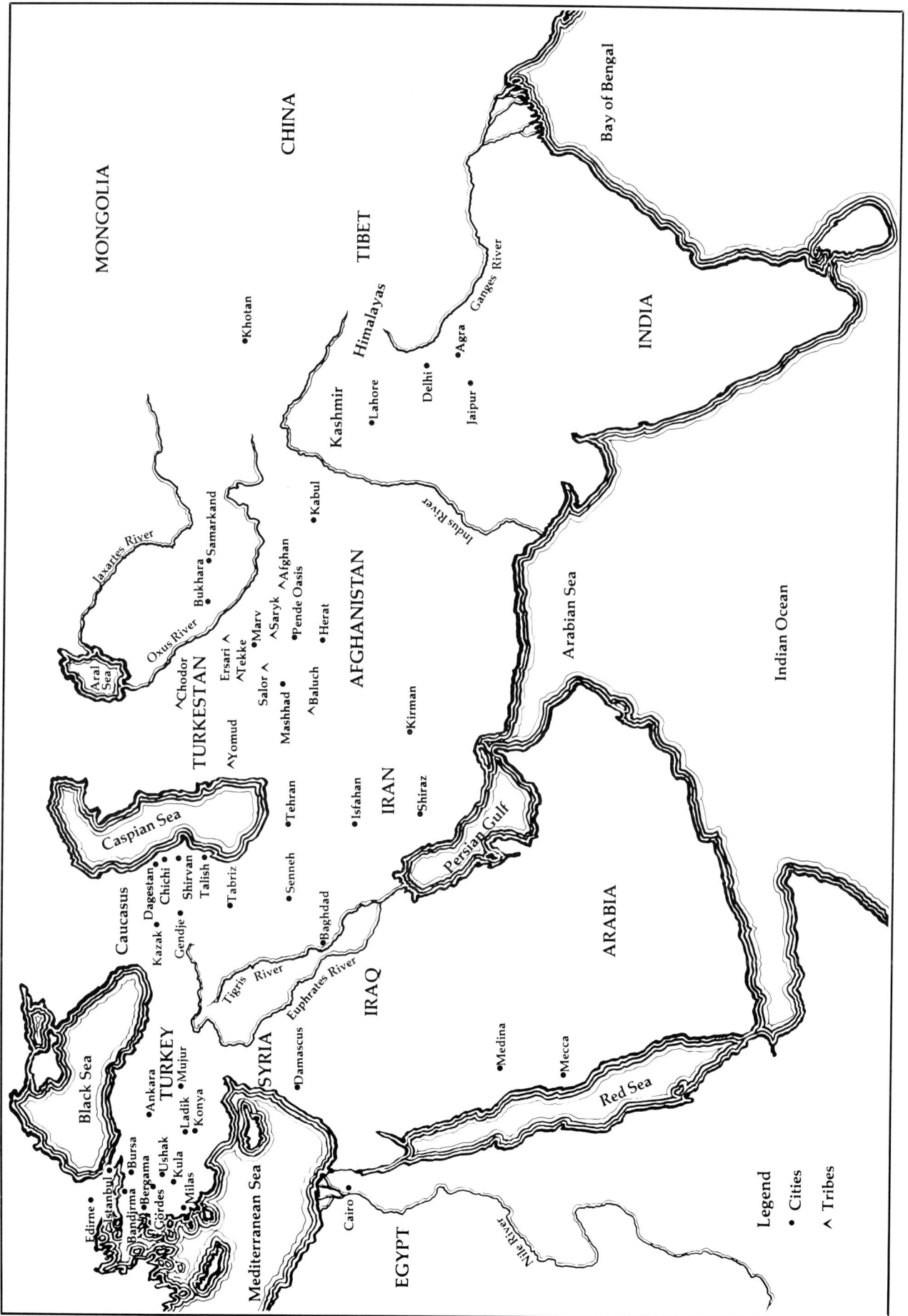

Figure 30—Map drawn by Ruth L. Fisher.

SELECTED BIBLIOGRAPHY

American Art Association
1925 *The V. and L. Benguiat Private Collection of Rare Old Rugs*, Sale Dec. 4, 5, New York.

Anonymous
1961 *Samples of the Old Turkish Carpets and Kilims*, Istanbul.

Beattie, May H.
1963 "Background to the Turkish Rug," *Oriental Art*, Vol. IX, No. 3, pp.3-10.
1968 "Coupled-Column Prayer Rugs," *Oriental Art*, Vol. XIV, No. 4, pp.243-258.
1972 *The Thyssen-Bornemisza Collection of Oriental Rugs*, Switzerland.

Bidder, Hans
1964 *Carpets from Eastern Turkestan*, Tübingen.

Bode, Wilhelm von, and Kühnel, Ernst
1958 *Antique Rugs from the Near East*, 4th ed., tr. by C.G. Ellis, Braunschweig.

Bogolubov, Andrei Andreyevich
1908 *Tapis de l'Asie Centrale*, St. Petersbourg.

Bogolyubov, Andrei Andreyevich
1973 *Carpets of Central Asia*, ed. by J.M.A. Thompson, England.

Breck, Joseph, and Morris, Frances
1923 *The James F. Ballard Collection of Oriental Rugs*, New York.

Cammann, Schuyler V.R.
1972 "Symbolic Meanings in Oriental Rug Patterns," *Textile Museum Journal*, Vol. III, No. 3, pp. 5-54.

Denny, Walter B.
1973 "Anatolian Rugs: An Essay on Method," *Textile Museum Journal*, Vol. III, No. 4, pp. 7-25.

Dickie, James
1972 "The Iconography of the Prayer Rug," *Oriental Art*, Vol. XVIII, No. 1, pp. 2-11.

Dilley, Arthur Urbane
1959 *Oriental Rugs and Carpets*, rev. by Maurice S. Dimand, New York.

Dimand, Maurice S.
1958 *A Handbook of Muhammadan Art*, 3rd ed., rev., New York.
1961 *Peasant and Nomad Rugs of Asia*, New York.
1973 with a chapter by Jean Mailey, *Rugs in the Metropolitan Museum of Art*, New York.

Ellis, Charles Grant
1963 "A Soumak-Woven Rug in a 15th Century International Style," *Textile Museum Journal*, Vol. I, No. 2, pp. 3-20.
1969 "The Ottoman Prayer Rugs," *Textile Museum Journal*, Vol. II, No. 4, pp. 5-22.

El Sadi, Subhi Mustafa
1929 "Antique Prayer Rugs from the Orient," *The Antiquarian*, Vol. XIII, No. 3, pp. 32-35.

Emery, Irene
1966 *The Primary Structure of Fabrics*, Washington, D.C.

Enderlein, Volkmar
1971 "Zwei Ägyptische Gebetsteppiche im Islamischen Museum," *Forschungen und Berichte, Staatliche Museen zu Berlin*, Band 13.

Erdmann, Kurt
1941 " 'The Art of Carpet Making,' in A Survey of Persian Art: Rezension," *Ars Islamica*, Vol. VIII, pp. 121-191.
1961 "Neuere Untersuchungen zur Frage der Kairener Teppiche," *Ars Orientalis*, Vol. IV, pp. 65-105.
1962 *Oriental Carpets*, 2nd ed., tr. by C.G. Ellis, New York.
1970 *Seven Hundred Years of Oriental Carpets*, ed. by Hanna Erdmann, tr. by M.H. Beattie and H. Herzog, Berkeley and Los Angeles.

Ettinghausen, Richard
1954 "Notes on the Lustreware of Spain: III The 'Khams' or Hand Symbol," *Ars Orientalis*, Vol. I, pp. 148-154.
1957 "New Light on Animal Carpets," *Aus der Welt der islamischen Kunst, Festschrift E. Kühnel*, ed. by R. Ettinghausen, pp. 93-116.
1966 *Treasures of Turkey: The Islamic Period*, Geneva.

1970 "Islamic Carpets: The Joseph V. McMullan Collection," *The Metropolitan Museum of Art Bulletin,* Vol. XXVIII.

Jones, H. McCoy
1969 *The Ersari and their Weavings,* Washington, D.C. (mimeograph).

Jones, Quill, and Plaxton, Iola
1928 "Tradition of the Prayer Rug," *The Antiquarian,* Vol. X, No. 1, pp. 60-64.

Kendrick, A.F. and Tattersall, C.E.C.
1922 *Hand-Woven Carpets Oriental & European,* New York.

Kühnel, Ernst, with technical analysis by Louisa Bellinger
1957 *Cairene Rugs and Others Technically Related: 15th-17th Century,* Washington, D.C.

Landolt, Hermann
1965 "Gedanken zum islamischen Gebetsteppich," *Festschrift Alfred Bühler,* ed. by C.A. Schmitz and R. Wildhaber, Basel, pp. 243-256.

Macey, R.E.G.
1961 *Oriental Prayer Rugs,* Leigh-on-Sea.

MacLean, J. Arthur, and Blair, Dorothy
1924 *Catalogue of Oriental Rugs in the Collection of James F. Ballard,* Indianapolis.

Mackie, Louise W.
1973 *The Splendor of Turkish Weaving,* Washington, D.C.

Mailey, Jean
1973 "Rugs of China and Chinese Turkestan," in M.S. Dimand, *Oriental Rugs in the Metropolitan Museum of Art,* New York.

Mann, T.
1914 *Der Islam: Monographien zur Weltgeschicht* Vol. 32, Leipzig.

McMullen, Joseph V.
1965 *Islamic Carpets,* New York.

Moshkova, W.G.
1970 *Carpets of the Late 19th and Early 20th Centuries* (in Russian), Tashkent.

Mostafa, Mohamed
1953 *Turkish Prayer Rugs,* Cairo.

Nicolas Sursock Museum
1963 *Exhibition of Oriental Carpets* (in Arabic, French, and English), Beirut.

Reed, Christopher Dunham
1966 *Turkoman Rugs,* Cambridge, Mass.

Renaissance Society at the University of Chicago
1973 *Islamic Prayer Rugs,* Chicago.

Sakisian, Arménag Bey
1931 "L'Inventaire des tapis de la mosquée Yeni-Djami de Stamboul," *Syria,* pp. 368-373.

Sarre, Friedrich
1908 *Ancient Oriental Carpets,* Leipzig.

Sarre, Friedrich, and Trenkwald, Hermann
1926 *Old Oriental Carpets,* tr. by A.F. Kendrick, Vienna and Leipzig.

Schlosser, Ignaz
1963 *The Book of Rugs Oriental and European,* New York.

Schmutzler, Emil
1933 *Altorientalische Teppiche in Siebenbürgen,* Leipzig.

Schürmann, Ulrich
n.d. *Caucasian Rugs,* Braunschweig.
1966 *Oriental Carpets,* London.
1969 *Central Asian Rugs,* Frankfurt.

The Textile Museum
1973 *Turkish Rugs from Private Collections,* Washington, D.C. (gallery guide, mimeograph).

Végh, J. de, and Layer, Ch.
1925 *Tapis Turcs: Provenant des églises et collections de Transylvanie,* Paris.

Welch, Stuart C.
1963 *The Art of Mughal India,* New York.

Yohe, Ralph S., and Jones, H. McCoy, eds.
1968 *Turkish Rugs,* Washington, D.C.

Zick, Johanna
1961 "Eine Gruppe von Gebetsteppichen und ihre Datierung," *Berliner Museen, Berichte aus den ehem. Preuss. Kunstsammlung,* N.F., Jg. 11, S. 6-14.

L.W.M.

Color Photography: Otto E. Nelson, New York, N.Y.: pls. I, IX, X, XI, XX, XXIII, XXVII, XXIX, XXX, XXXI, XXXIV, XXXVIII, XL, XLII; Raymond Schwartz, Washington, D.C.: pls. III, VI, XII, XIII, XIX, XXVIII, XXXII, XXXIII, XXXV, XXXVII, XXXIX, XLI; and supplied by The Walters Art Gallery, The St. Louis Art Museum, and Edmund de Unger.

Design: Peter D. Tasi & Kathy Jungjohann
Typography: Mid-Atlantic Photo Composition, Inc.
Printing: Stephenson Lithograph Inc.